Milwa ee Walks

20 Choice Walks in a Classy City

by

Cari Taylor-Carlson

Serendipity Ink   Milwaukee, Wisconsin

Serendipity Ink
P.O. Box 17163
Milwaukee, WI 53217

Library of Congress Catalog Card Number: 91-90320

First Printing 1991
Second Printing 1992

Cover design, maps and illustrations: Lynne Bergschultz,
    Stablegraphics Studio
Editing and graphic production: Montgomery Media, Inc.

ISBN 0-9629452-0-X

Feb. 20, 1993

Dad:
    Something for you +
Pat to do between
baseball games this
summer! Have a
spectacular birthday!

    In ♥ + ☮,
        Molly

For my parents
Buzz and Audrey Ferry
who taught me to see with my heart

Freeways and Major Streets

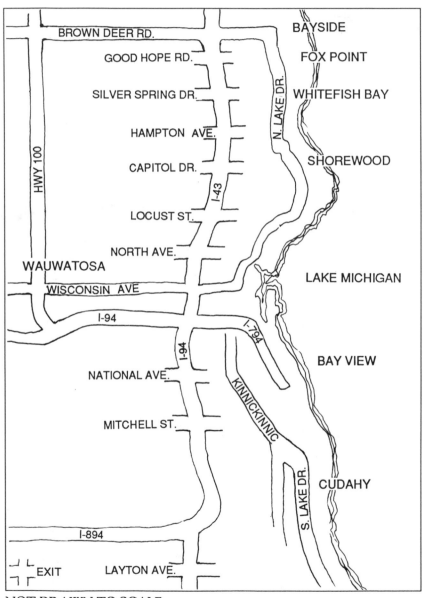

BROWN DEER RD.

GOOD HOPE RD.

SILVER SPRING DR.

HAMPTON AVE.

CAPITOL DR.

LOCUST ST.

NORTH AVE.

WISCONSIN AVE

I-94

NATIONAL AVE.

MITCHELL ST.

I-894

LAYTON AVE.

EXIT

HWY 100

I-43

I-94

WAUWATOSA

BAYSIDE

FOX POINT

WHITEFISH BAY

N. LAKE DR.

SHOREWOOD

LAKE MICHIGAN

I-794

BAY VIEW

KINNICKINNIC

CUDAHY

S. LAKE DR.

NOT DRAWN TO SCALE

Table of Contents

Acknowledgments

I wish to thank the team at Montgomery Media who gave me great support and I appreciate Sue Montgomery's enthusiasm for the project, Priya Sengupta's creative competence, and Mary Huntington's editing skills. Thanks to the people who contributed their expertise and time: Laurie Otto, Shirley du Fresne McArthur, David Lagerman, Becky Crawford, and Mary Goode; thanks to Bill Nelson who encouraged me to write, and a special thank you to Lynne Bergschultz whose friendship, patience, and many talents made this book possible.

C.T-C.

Introduction

The best way to see Milwaukee is on foot. The only way to really get to know an area will always be up close—eyeball to eyeball—where you can reach out and touch the buildings, beaches, parks, restaurants, and shops—the list is endless. Of course, don't miss the local residents! Milwaukee's colorful history, filled with wave after wave of hardworking immigrants, is still visible today in local neighborhoods. Even though the descendants of those early settlers may be long gone, they left many traces behind them.

Polish duplexes remind us of their extraordinary thrift. South Side churches stand testimony to pockets of immigrants whose labors of love built lasting treasures, and a visit to a shop like Bits of Britain will bring to mind the original Bay View settlers from the British Isles.

Milwaukee isn't San Francisco, yet it's filled with turn-of-the-century charm and a lakefront that sets us apart as a magnificent city on a major body of sparkling blue water. Seven walks in this book follow the lake from Fox Point north to south of downtown in Cudahy. Lake Michigan dominates Milwaukee today just as it did 155 years ago when the first white men arrived from the East, determined to build a city.

Early settlers knew they'd stumbled onto a special place. In June 1835, the first steamboat passengers landed at Milwaukee where they found a sheltered bay and three streams that drain most of southeastern Wisconsin. Alongside the Milwaukee and Menomonee Rivers and Kinnickinnic Creek, they found Potawatomi Indian villages and a few cabins built by fur traders. The Potawatomi called this place *Mah-au-wauke-seepe*, which means "gathering place by the river."

Not all the early residents were charmed. In a letter to Mrs. Joseph Slidell in Detroit (quoted in the *Milwaukee Journal* in 1946), George Pinckney wrote:

Dear Jane,
Joe has got me out here, and here I am and a more miserable God-forsaken place I never saw. The town, or what there is of it, is right in the middle of a swamp. You can't go half a mile in any direction without getting into the water. It's a pretty deep mudhole all over. The river is a great thing I expect, but when you have to paddle over it three or four times a day in a dugout, it is a nuisance.

This is the swamp Solomon Juneau, Byron Kilbourn and George H. Walker found when they arrived in the 1830s and promoted the lands associated with the names "Juneautown," east of the river, "Kilbourntown," west of the river, and "Walker's Point," south of downtown.

In those early years, most of the settlers were Yankees who came by water from the northeastern states. Travel across the Great Lake route was convenient. Next came the Irish, driven across the ocean by the potato famines of the 1840s. They were followed by Norwegians and Germans and by 1860, Milwaukee's population topped 45,000. More than half were European immigrants. The rest is history, and as you stroll the neighborhoods, you'll feel a strong tie to the past and may come to view Milwaukee as the classic American "melting pot."

Today, tucked away in greater Milwaukee, are numerous neighborhoods where a walk will introduce you properly to their unique attractions. Each walk holds surprises and opportunities to observe firsthand our diverse communities. I'm proud to live in a midwestern city where limiting a walking book to just twenty walks turned into a challenge.

Welcome to Milwaukee! There's plenty to see and do. Step out in comfortable shoes and enjoy the city. I hope you have as much fun walking about these streets as I did plotting, planning, mapping, walking, and writing about them.

C.T-C.

"It is not true that Milwaukee is exactly like every other American city, only more so. It has a distinct personality, although not one that is as immediately apparent as San Francisco's foggy cosmopolitanism or Chicago's hopeful cynicism. Milwaukee is a place that grows on you gradually, like a beer belly . . . But such wistful delusions of municipal grandeur are not typical of Milwaukeeans. Except for an occasional politician or a public relations man, he is not a hometown booster. He regards his city with wry affection that is unmixed with any illusion about its glamor, the way a husband looks on a wife who'll never be asked to pose for Playboy but who's a darn good cook."

This Is Milwaukee, *Robert W. Wells, 1970*

No. 1 Chic Shop Walk

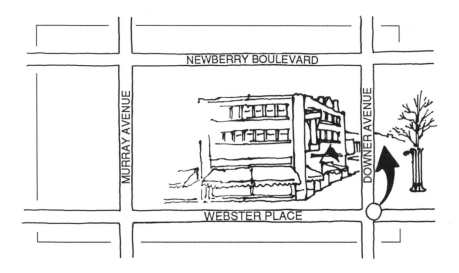

Distance
1.4 miles

How to Begin
Take the Locust Street Exit east from I-43 north. Drive east on
Locust to Oakland Avenue, go south on Oakland to Webster Place,
and east on Webster to the corner of Webster and Downer Avenue.

Introduction
Sensible shoes don't belong here. Funky students, leftover
hippies, and carefully styled matrons pour in and out of
Downer Avenue establishments each day. Wanted—sidewalk
cafes for front-row seats to the best eclectic style show in town.

Downer Avenue is pure East Side. Originally called Glen
Avenue, it was renamed in 1898 for Judge Jason Downer, the
first editor of the *Milwaukee Sentinel*.

This Avenue, small-town hub of the chic East Side, indulges shoppers for three blocks from the intersection at Webster Place to Newberry Boulevard. This long-standing diverse area is home to a small, colorful community, and a great place to explore on a Saturday morning. Bring money.

This chic shop walk starts at the **corner of Webster and Downer** at Webster's Cafe and Bookstore, where the outside logo "Feed Your Imagination" should include "and Your Stomach." A bowl of their thick soup *du jour* served with a bread basket will send walkers off with satisfied tummies. An ever-changing selection of shops and restaurants line both sides of Downer. Some, like the Chancery, FootGear, and Ma Jolie, are new kids on the block, while old-timers include Paperworks, the Book Bay, Sendiks, and the Coffee Trader.

The Coffee Trader is the best place to be seen. Guests sit at small tables (on an occasional rickety chair) surrounded by Cream City brick walls, hanging ferns, potted plants, open rafters, ceiling fans, classical music, and other chic people. The coffee's great too.

Across the street at the Book Bay, the scene is crowded. This children's bookstore, jammed with books and decorated with green and yellow polka dots, hanging umbrellas, and a green frog, encourages youngsters to look and touch. A kid-sized table with kid-sized benches where books are casually left open for browsing proved irresistible when a young family entered. "Look, here's a table!" rang out.

Across the street, kitchen gourmets love Sendik's Fruit, Meat, and Fish Market. Flowers line the sidewalk in season, and all year the sweet scent from blossoms inside greets shoppers at the entrance. If the flowers don't detain you, the produce will.

A block farther up the street to the west, turn left on
Newberry Boulevard and shopping bustle will be replaced by
boulevard bustle. Traffic, college students kicking and throw-
ing balls, bikers, rollerblade skaters in black Lycra tights,
mothers pushing strollers accompanied by kids and dogs, and
an increasing legion of recreational walkers have taken over
Newberry Boulevard. East Siders thrive on diversity, and
Newberry won't disappoint walkers looking for an unusual
parade of homes.

According to Shirley du Fresne McArthur, curator of the
North Point Historical Society, it must have been quiet one
hundred years ago when Olmsted, Olmsted & Eliot envisioned
Newberry as a boulevard and promenade to link Lake(side)
Park to River(side) Park. " Substantial homes were designed
and built over a thirty-year period to delight the eye of pedestrians and carriage riders," she says. " Architects were eager to
demonstrate their creative efforts to establish reputations and
the work of many is represented between Lake Drive and
Oakland Avenue. They avoided a strict historic orientation
and relied upon eclectic interpretation of a style, using various
motifs—sometimes reaching a happy solution and sometimes
missing their mark. (Some examples include a Tudor Revival
home at 2530, a Russell Barr Williamson home in the Frank
Lloyd Wright Prairie style at 2430, a Tudor Revival home with
Queen Anne elements at 2415, an Italian Renaissance adaptation with Mediterranean elements at 2404, at 2331 a free
interpretation of Colonial Revival with a French feeling, a
home with decorative Italian Renaissance features at 2229 and
an adaptation of Tudor English architecture at 2122.)

"The architectural styles on Newberry follow the social
patterns of the period. As the people prospered, they wanted to
spend their wealth on grander homes. The houses we live in
reflect our personalities more than we realize. The English,

French, Prairie and Italian styles were the primary influences on Newberry, a microcosm of the styles that were influencing most Americans of the same period."

At Murray Avenue, turn left and walk one block south to Trep-Art. Here they stock enough Lycra to outfit every firm body under thirty in greater Milwaukee. Someone must have thrown a hand grenade into a rainbow and split it into a billion colors to make the displays at Trep-Art.

Beyond Lycra, they stock shoes for folk, jazz, tap, and ballroom dancing as well as for ballet and gymnastics. If you keep going though doors, you'll find the room where they sell theatrical supplies and little girls' dreams. Women will recall playing dress-up in Trep-Art's "All That Glitters" shop, and if it glitters, it's surely here. Sequins, feather boas of all colors, ribbons, satins, lace, tulle, net, fill the room. You can almost hear the late Greta Garbo mumuring soft words of endearment to a screen lover as she flings a feather wrap from this room over her slinky shoulders.

From Trep-Art, it's a quick walk south on Murray to Webster. Turn east on Webster to return to the bookstore and cafe for a cookie and a sweet end to a chic stroll.

"After the village's eastern and western halves had been consolidated, the authorities started passing new rules, among them one that forbade hogs to run at large. In 1840 this was considered a ridiculous example of bureaucratic interference in the natural state of urban life by many citizens. They pointed out that the hogs provided an efficient garbage disposal system and didn't charge a cent."
This Is Milwaukee, *Robert W. Wells, 1970*

No. 2 Gentrifying Neighborhood Walk

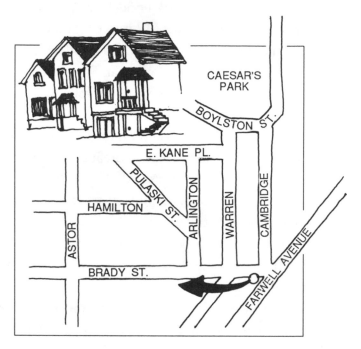

Distance
1.7 miles

How to Begin
Take North Avenue east from I-43 north to Holton Street. Travel south on Holton across the Milwaukee River until it intersects with Brady Street. Drive east on Brady to Farwell Avenue.

Introduction
"Home for sale in rapidly gentrifying Brady Street neighborhood"—this is realtor's rhetoric describing a community that was formerly Polish and Irish and most recently, Italian.

Today, much of the ethnic character has faded from Brady along with the hippie culture of the '70s, and in their place is a smorgasbord of shops lining a six-block area from Farwell to Astor. Walkers will find antiques, flowers, hardware, pets, recycled clothes, funerals, darts, plumbing, and janitorial supplies for sale here. What they won't find is a fast-food restaurant. Instead, a stir-fry of characteristics lingers from past and present residents.

Start walking at the corner of Brady and Farwell in front of the upscale East Towne Plaza. This newness seems inappropriate here, for it's a far cry from the former Cream City brick, Queen Anne-style apartment building that occupied the site from the 1890s until progress demolished it in the 1980s.

Down the block, Nicolo's Sicilian Pub and Ristorante Internazionale has become a sad corpse of its former self—a broken-down building with "No Trespassing" posted on the door. Only the fancy grillwork fence on Brady Street and the Cream City brick wall hint of bygone days when Nicolo's served elegant Italian dinners and the best deep-fried eggplant in town. Milwaukee lost a fine bistro when the doors closed in 1986.

The Italian ambience moved across the street to Mimma's Cafe. Rated by *Milwaukee* Magazine as a "Best of Milwaukee," this tiny cafe prepares an ambitious selection of pasta asciutta, gourmet pizza, calzones, and panini imbottiti. Dishes such as Lumachetti alla Kafara (pasta with fresh peas with white or red sauce), have given Mimma's a reputation for excellence. In fact, in April 1991 they won another award. The Academy Awards of the restaurant industry rated Mimma's one of the 50 top Italian restaurants in the United States and #5 in the midwest. After a two-block walk, a rest is premature, but remember to return to float away with some Italian music and to remember an Italian Brady Street.

Italians weren't the original settlers, however, for the Polish and Irish had come first. In the 1800s when industry expanded along the Milwaukee River, work on railroads, in tanneries and ice houses brought immigrants looking for a new life in a new world. St. Hedwig's Parish, up the street at Humboldt and Brady, became a center for the Polish community and the first of several churches built to accommodate the swelling Polish population.

Many of these early settlers came from the Kaszuby region on Poland's Baltic coast and they were known locally as "Kaszubs." In 1874, there were 250 of these families at St. Hedwig's, where they came to hear sermons in their native Polish. Gradually, the original Polish and Irish communities declined as the people become more affluent and moved to newer, less crowded parts of the city.

The Italians arrived in the 1920s, moving north from the Old Third Ward to the then rural East Side. Two establishments remain from those good old days—Peter Sciortino's Bakery, where they make "melt in your mouth" cannoli daily and across the street, the Glorioso Brothers Co. grocery store which offers a wide range of Italian specialties and meats as well as Sciortino's cannoli on Saturdays.

Although it's long gone, in 1894, the Children's Free Hospital was established on Brady Street. Seven women founded the hospital, paying thirty dollars a month rent for a small house which held ten beds and one nurse, who received a monthly salary of twenty-five dollars. Those industrious founders made the draperies and bedsheets, and polished the floors themselves. Twenty-three children were served the first year.

Turn right on Astor, then right on Hamilton and right

again on to Pulaski Street. As you walk on Pulaski, look for signs of Polish immigrants on this street where they brought their intense desire for home ownership in the late 1800s. The hardworking Polish-Americans often built small frame houses, and as they became more affluent, they raised the frame up off the foundation and built a second unit in the half-basement beneath to provide more room for a growing family or a source of rental income. Now that's classic, efficient use of limited space!

You'll find several of these arrangements along Pulaski where the street is narrow and crowded. At the bend, look at the Cream City brick building at 1729-31. It looks like an ordinary boxy brick building until you notice the leaded glass window on the first floor. This building began as a stable and in 1905 when the Suminski Funeral Home took over, the window was added.

Turn left on Arlington to see two more examples of basement duplexes at 1748 and 1752. Farther up the block at 1819-21, watch for a turn-of-the-century building that shows how early entrepreneurs combined residential and commercial use before the onset of zoning regulations. An unusual Polish flat at 1860-62, built in 1885, combines Italianate with Polish thrift.

Turn right on Kane Place and look straight ahead to a lineup of well-maintained vintage homes on Warren Street. The Cream City duplex at 1900-02 used to be the rectory of St. Hedwig's Parish. The thrifty Poles even recycled buildings; when the parish built a new rectory on Humboldt Avenue, the old one was sold and moved here.

Turn left on Warren and follow it to Boylston Street and Caesar's Park. The park could use a clean-up and some "neighborhood pride." Named after local resident Caesar Paikowski, it overlooks the Milwaukee River, and walkers can see across to more Polish settlements built west of the river after the Humboldt Street Bridge spanned it in 1883.

Below the park, the North Avenue Dam, built in 1840, used to divide north and south on the river. To the south in the late 1800s were sawmills, flour mills, furniture factories, breweries, and tanneries. The river banks north of the dam were lined with swimming schools, canoe clubs, and amusement parks.

A cement walk goes down to the river from the park where patient fishermen bring up suckers, carp, and trout. "Bet we'll have a late night snack, 'cause my mom's already fixed supper" was overheard in summertime as three young boys hauled a net filled with fifty pounds of fish up the steep hillside above the river. Their interest in the "late night snack" didn't extend to the ones they dropped along the way.

In May it's showtime when spawning fish swimming upstream fling themselves again and again against the frothing current. Like Sisyphus pushing his rock, they refuse to acknowledge eternal disappointment. If your nose can overlook old beer cans and Milwaukee River "perfume," this is a good place to watch an urban sunset across a city river.

From Caesar's Park, **a short walk south on Cambridge** leads back to the beginning of this walk through a "gentrifying" Milwaukee neighborhood.

"Lieutenant James Gorrell, British commander at Green Bay, mentioned 'Milwacky' in 1761, upholding the early tradition of never spelling the community's name the same twice. Exactly what the Indians themselves called the place is in some doubt. 'Mahn-a-wauk-ee-seepe' which meant 'gathering place by the river' is the version preferred by most Milwaukeeans, although one nineteenth century writer claimed Milwaukee was originally 'Mee-lee-wauk-ee.' He said this meant 'stinking river' in Winnebago, indicating that the decision of Lake Michigan alewives to see Milwaukee and die is not a modern phenomenon at all."

This Is Milwaukee, Robert W. Wells, 1970

"Milwaukee had one important asset, however—a plentiful supply of Yankees who had a talent for selling real estate that was still covered by two feet of swamp water. It also had the advantage of a climate that could be depended upon to keep the marsh frozen for a considerable portion of the year."

This Is Milwaukee, Robert W. Wells, 1970

No. 3 Lake Loop Walk

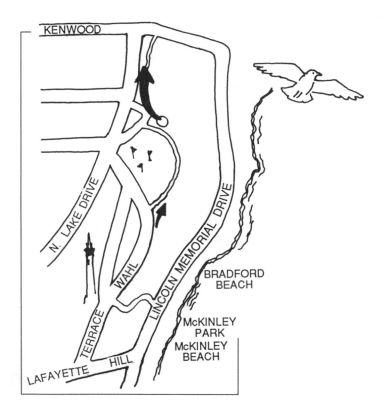

Distance
4.4 miles

How to Begin
From I-43 north take the Locust Street exit and drive east to North Lake Drive. Go one block south on Lake Drive to the entrance to Lake Park. Leave the car in the lot by the pavilion.

Introduction
Lake Park, one of Milwaukee's first parks is sometimes crowded and never disappointing. It has a population that includes

tennis players, golfers, walkers, joggers, babies, old people, lovers, newspaper readers, and a steady stream of sun worshipers. On this walk you can dive into historic Milwaukee along Lake Michigan's bluffs or you can simply turn your head eastward to the lake. Most of the time the walk follows the perimeter of Lake Park from the pavilion, along Bradford Beach, past McKinley tennis courts, along Terrace Avenue and back through the park again.

Start at the pavilion by the parking lot. Come on a summer Sunday and watch men dressed in crisp white roll a small white ball on a manicured lawn. Lawn bowling has been around since the twelfth century, and it looks easy until you notice that each time they roll the ball, it starts out in a straight line toward the target and ends in a wiggle. The target, also a white ball, is smaller and called a "jack." The closer the ball gets to the jack, the more points awarded the player.

Down by the end of the lawn bowling arena, there's a big old beech tree. In springtime, put an ear to it on a windy day and listen carefully. You might hear it gurgle.

From the tree, walk toward Lake Drive on the park road and turn right. Now you're in the middle of Lake Park, 123 acres acquired from private landowners in 1890 and designed by Frederick Law Olmsted, known for his role in designing New York's Central Park. Lake Park is one of Milwaukee's oldest parks.

Along the way, notice several shagbark hickory trees— they can be recognized easily by their shaggy bark. An interesting study could be made of the different shapes of the trees that stand between the bus turnaround and Lincoln Memorial Drive. Cones, ovals, circles, squares, rectangles, trees with curvilinear branches, trees with ruler-straight branches and trees with drooping branches all grow right here. Someone with foresight planted this tree garden for us to enjoy.

At Lincoln Memorial Drive, turn right and walk down the hill to the bottom and a great view of downtown Milwaukee. The skyline, dominated by the First Wisconsin Building and accented by Bradford Beach, looks like a Renaissance study in depth perception.

Along the beach watch out for gulls, hungry for scraps and not shy about joining people looking for rays. Despite warnings about sunbathing, on a hot day sunshine reflects off sleek, oiled bodies and the air is pungent with Coppertone.

Two parking lots vibrate from boom boxes tuned to different stations, adding to the summertime chaos. Once you're past the North Point Snack Bar where a McDonald's was vetoed a few years ago, **cross over and pick up the new walking trail on the east side of Lincoln Memorial.** This walkway skirts a boulder field where unfortunately, fools with spray paint guns are beginning to decorate the landscape with graffiti.

At the McKinley tennis courts the walk goes up—up the hill where summer bike racers compete—to the top of the bluff and Lafayette Place.

Before you climb the hill, notice the Milwaukee Metropolitan Sewage District's Milwaukee River Flushing Station. Forty thousand gallons per minute of Lake Michigan water are pumped into the Milwaukee River just below the North Avenue dam. This is done to ensure a high concentration of oxygen in the river at a place where algal growth would otherwise deplete the oxygen needed by fish. When the flushing station was built in 1888, it was the largest in the world.

On the top of the bluff, turn right and follow Terrace Avenue. At 2220 is Villa Terrace, a museum of decorative arts operated by the Milwaukee Art Museum in a stunning Italian

Renaissance home built in 1923 by L. R. Smith, son of industrialist A. O. Smith. The Smith children collected stones from the beach for the mosaic floor in the courtyard.

At the intersection by St. Mary's Hospital, walk to the right along the bluff on Wahl Avenue. There's lots to see at this busy corner. There's the Hospital, founded in 1848 at the corner of Wells and Jackson downtown and called Saint John's Infirmary, until it was relocated in 1858 under its present name. In the 1850s, this was a busy place during the smallpox and cholera epidemics.

Notice the North Point Water Tower, 175 feet tall, made of limestone and erected in 1873. It holds a pipe that was used to relieve pressure on the city's water main that began on the shore below. It no longer functions except as a sentimental landmark.

Follow Wahl along the bluff and angle right back into the park at Belleview Place. After you cross the bridge, you'll soon come to the still-operating Northpoint Lighthouse which uses 1,300,000 candlepower and is visible for twenty-five miles.

Follow the path past the par three golf hole back to the parking lot where you can sit awhile and enjoy the ambience of a city park and a fresh Lake Michigan breeze.

"We came to Milwaukee where we were to pass a fortnight or more. This place is most beautifully situated. A little river with romantic banks passes through the town. The bank of the lake is here a bold bluff eighty feet in height. From its summit, you enjoy a noble outlook on the lake."

A Summer on the Lakes, Margaret Fuller, 1843

"Milwaukee clubwomen followed the example of Pittsburgh and Chicago in securing the passage of an anti-spitting ordinance in 1904. Street cars and public buildings were now forbidden territory for the indulgence of this traditionally American habit."

Milwaukee, The History of a City, Bayrd Still, 1948

"By the time Milwaukee had become a city, the settlers had already managed to pollute their environment . . . Acting Mayor Smith signed an ordinance making it illegal for anyone to bring such disease as cholera to Milwaukee . . . It turns out, however, that the ordinance was ineffective as most bacteria in those days were unable to read."

This Is Milwaukee, Robert W. Wells, 1970

No. 4 Painted Lady Walk

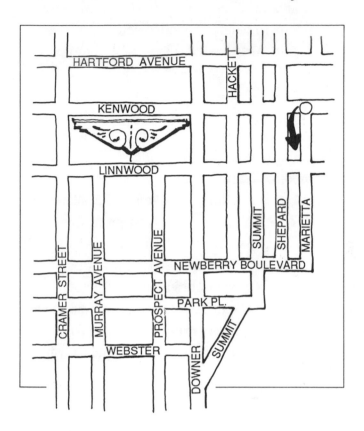

Distance
4 miles

How to Begin
*Take the Locust Street exit off I-43 north and travel east to
Marietta Street. Turn left and drive two blocks north to Kenwood
and park at the corner of Kenwood and Marietta.*

Introduction
Milwaukee has two historic mansion districts, one on the
lower East Side and one on the near North Side between

Wisconsin Avenue and Highland Boulevard. This walk, just north of the heart of the East Side mansions, showcases more modest homes, built about the same time. It's fascinating to note what time has done to neighborhoods. Here it has been kind, for you'll walk past thirty "painted ladies," and more blossom every year.

They're hard to miss—these Victorian homes edged with decorative fringes in rainbow colors. "Victorian" (as used here) is a catch-all term used to describe a variety of styles that flourished in the United States during the reign of England's Queen Victoria (1837-1901), with the greatest profusion appearing after 1870. Victorian builders borrowed liberally from Italian, French, Tudor, and even Oriental traditions. Their structures were marked by visual variety and elaborate detail—a reaction to the rigidly classical styles of the previous period. The Victorian Age was also a time of rapid expansion in the United States and the picturesque styles came to symbolize the romantic spirit of the times.

Victorian architecture mirrored the rise of new technologies. Pre-cut lumber and machine-made nails replaced the laborious methods of earlier years. The mechanical scroll saw eliminated the need for wood carvers. As a result, design possibilities were more numerous and "gingerbread" was more widely available. According to the *Discover Milwaukee Catalog*, published by the Milwaukee Department of City Development in 1986:

> Milwaukee neighborhoods settled during the Victorian era are still the most diverse in the city. Most residents lived within a mile or two of downtown at the time and this density meant that owners and factory workers often shared the same blocks. Elaborate Queen Anne

and Italianate homes, complete with marble fireplaces, wrought-iron balustrades, and stained glass windows, were built just down the street from small cottages with scrollwork in the eaves and above the windows.

Scattered among the single family homes here are many duplexes built about the same time. They represent Milwaukeeans' well-documented thrift. They're good-sized homes, usually built by working- class families, who needed tenant help to meet the monthly mortgage payments. Their diverse styles include touches of Victorian elegance and some are noted on this "painted lady" walk.

Whether they're single-family homes or duplexes, the unifying theme here is rehabilitation. This is a neighborhood on the rise. It's always been a good place to live and a safe place to walk, and this elegant parade of painted ladies adds frosting to the cake.

Start at the corner of Marietta Avenue and Kenwood Boulevard. Here are the ladies' addresses:

2937 Marietta Avenue
2736 Shepard Avenue
2737 Shepard Avenue
2732 Shepard Avenue
621 Summit Avenue
2614-16 Prospect Avenue
2628 Prospect Avenue
2640 Prospect Avenue
2919 Prospect Avenue
2953-55 Murray Avenue
Southwest corner of Murray Avenue and
Newberry Boulevard
2762 Cramer Street

2920 Cramer Street
3039-41 Cramer Street
3212 Downer Avenue
The block between Hartford Avenue and Kenwood Boulevard
on Hackett is a veritable rehab row with too many to list.
2716-18 Kenwood Boulevard
2726 Kenwood Boulevard
2928 Kenwood Boulevard

Thinking about rehabing an older home? You've just
explored a lifesize catalog of possibilities!

Start at Marietta Avenue and Kenwood Boulevard.
South on Marietta
Right on Newberry Boulevard
Left on Shepard Avenue
Right on Park Place
Left on Summit Avenue
Hard right on Downer Avenue
Left on Webster Place
Right on Prospect Avenue
Left on Linnwood Avenue
Left on Murray Avenue
Right on Park Place
Right on Cramer Street
Right on Hartford Avenue
(detour right one-half block here to 3212 Downer Avenue)
Right on Hackett Avenue
Left on Kenwood Boulevard

No. 5 Riverwest Art Walk

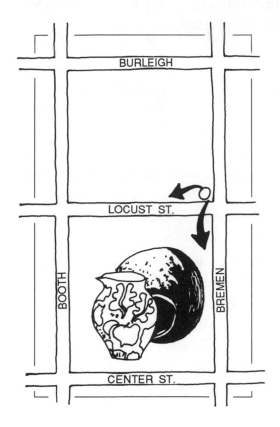

Distance
1.5 miles

How to Begin
Take the Locust Street exit off I-43 north and drive east on Locust to Bremen Street. The walk starts at the corner of Locust and Bremen.

Introduction
Many artists work in Riverwest and show their works else- where. With the exception of Woodland Pattern, the galleries

on this art walk have been open for only a few years, most since 1985. Perhaps more artists will follow the lead of potter Marnie Elbaum at 2711-13 Bremen and begin welcoming customers to their studios.

Riverwest, one of Milwaukee's most diverse neighborhoods, originally housed mill workers in the 1850s. Then Polish families moved in, many from across the river in the late 1800s, and they built the flats, cottages, and duplexes we see today. Later, affluent members of the German community built summer homes close to the river. As you walk, notice the character of the homes in this interesting turn-of-the-century neighborhood.

From Bremen, walk west to 800 Locust to see Stone Age Jewelry. Here, owner Lionel Minden III buys unfinished stones from which to create his jewelry. The cost of each piece will be partly based on the weight of the rocks Minden sells by the ounce; thus, this handmade jewelry can be sold at a reasonable price. Stone Age Jewelry has been recognized by *Milwaukee Magazine* twice, once in 1987 for "Cheap Stuff" and again in 1988 for "Best of . . . Jewelry."

Just beyond Stone Age, at 720 East Locust, Woodland Pattern is easily recognized by a street-side mural. Here you'll find a vast collection of small press books. Owner Ann Kingsbury invites browsers to settle into a cozy chair and sample a selection of the hundreds, maybe thousands, of one-of-a-kind books. Don't come to buy a best seller, or a business or pop psychology text, but you're likely to find the perfect book for the art connoisseur on your list.

Walk back on Locust to Bremen and wander south to 2711-13, where potter Marnie Elbaum opens her studio to the public Tuesday-Friday afternoons and Saturdays from 11-4.

Her studio looks like what it is, a working artist's space, and Marnie says, "The customers who come here have an appreciation of a handmade craft made by a real human." Her pottery is functional stoneware glazed in rich tones of black, brown, ivory, and blue.

Across the street at 833 Center, Artistry Studio Gallery looks more like an antique store or a corner of someone's attic than an art gallery until you notice the contemporary crafts. Artist and proprietor Susan Alexander has assembled a fascinating collection. One of her artists on display repairs old hats, decorates them with ribbons, uses them as models for drawings, and when she's done, she sells them. Susan Alexander works at many different crafts. At Christmas, she makes ceramic gingerbread houses that are lit inside with candles.

Turn right on Center and right again on Booth. Then turn right on Burleigh and look for the Silver Paper Gallery at 800 Burleigh. This small 1990 newcomer owned by Todd Groskopf focuses on Wisconsin artists who have not shown locally or have not had a one-person show. Artists who exhibit here may be unknown today and in demand tomorrow.
Turn right one last time on Bremen to walk back to Locust.

These Riverwest galleries are not on the walking tour but they are often willing to open by appointment:

Wright Street Gallery
922 East Wright

Cindy Crigler Studio
2611 North Booth

Riverwest Studio
800 East Clarke

Neon Artist Al Blankscien
832 East Auer

No. 6 Maritime Coast Walk

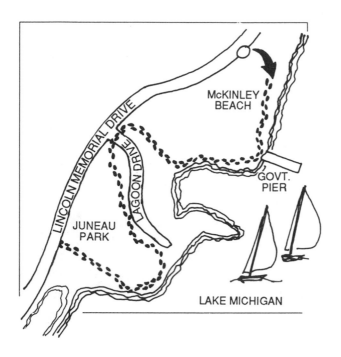

Distance
2 miles

How to Begin
Take I-794 east, and exit at Lincoln Memorial Drive. Head north on Lincoln Memorial past the lagoon and the Marina to McKinley tennis courts on the west side of the street. The walk begins at the McKinley Beach sign just beyond the tennis courts on Lincoln Memorial Drive.

Introduction
A municipal landfill project, completed in 1929, created for

Milwaukee one of the longest and most beautiful stretches of lakefront in urban America. The dual purpose of the project was to create public recreational space and to halt erosion from storms coming off Lake Michigan. For a delightful stroll in any season, explore Milwaukee's coast where sand, rock, sailboats, shimmering water, and plenty of activity color the landscape.

Bring the family and start in the sandbox at McKinley Beach on Lincoln Memorial Drive. Jump aboard the boat where kids of all ages can climb and explore and enjoy visions of grandeur as captain of the ship.

Here's a small harbor surrounded by sand, part of the reconstruction of the area after Lake Michigan reclaimed chunks of the landfill in 1987.

From this little jewel of a harbor, face downtown and walk through the parking lot and onto the concrete pier, known as Government Pier, constructed by the Army Corps of Engineers. Bring the kids, but leave bikes and dogs behind. It's been said that "fools' names, like fools' faces, are often seen in public places," and there must be a few in this area, for "John and Heidi" and others have attempted to immortalize themselves by writing their names on the stone in hot pink calligraphy.

Tenacious members of the plant kingdom are growing right beside the gaudy signatures. A fuzzy mullein plant two inches high has forced a sprout between concrete and metal. Here's a pioneer, determined to beat the odds and to flourish in hostile circumstances.

Further out on the pier, more graffiti dominate the view with heartfelt statements, proclamations of eternal love, and enlightened signs of an environmental conscience. Scattered along the way are fisherfolk, settled into chairs with radios and stoves, looking serene, and not terribly concerned about whether or not the fish are biting. "Where can you get better fresh air than here?" seemed to be the prevailing sentiment.

A metal wall near the end blocks further progress and it's time to turn around. The view is stunning. The eye is drawn to the south, downtown and beyond to a harbor filled with boats. There might be a lone kayak outside the harbor, skimming the waves and looking like a leaf accidently blown onto the lake's surface. You can see all the way past the Hoan Bridge and down the South Milwaukee lakeshore to Bay View. Behind you, pancake stacks of apartments and Milwaukee mansions line the bluff, and dead ahead is Lake Michigan, open water, and infinity.

After leaving the pier, walk to the Marina Restaurant where, during the season, they sell a limited menu of soda, ice cream, candy bars, and sandwiches. It's a great place to sit at a picnic table on a lazy summer afternoon and watch the marine world pass in the harbor.

The pace slows to a crawl here and the "fast lane" is easily forgotten amidst the scavenging gulls. Boat fumes, a murmur of voices from a nearby poker game, the metallic tinkle of buoys, and a fresh lake breeze fill all one's senses. Sometimes the entertainment includes drivers who get too close to the lake at the boat launch and slip into the algae instead. It's a good show, watching their futile attempts to extricate themselves from the slippery goo. Eventually a tow truck will arrive to end the agony of embarassment.

From the restaurant, head south through the parking lot past the Milwaukee Yacht Club back to Lincoln Memorial Drive. Head south again, then turn left on the service road for a view across the channel at the yacht club boats and a look at some of Milwaukee's flashiest yachts. Occasionally, a boat like the *Sea and H* from Boca Raton comes to call, dwarfing local craft with its presidential yacht-like demeanor.

From here, cross the concrete steps at the battered and deserted U.S. Coast Guard Station and walk through another parking lot past a few hundred more boats. Names like *High Anxiety, Misprint, Contentment, No Regrets,* and *Scrooge II* hint of private stories.

Continue following the lake and the boats until you come to a small cluster of buildings. To the left is a small building with red trim where the Milwaukee Community Sailing Center has its headquarters. You'll also find a kite shop, a bicycle rental shop, and a place to rent roller skates and blades. Please note the very sturdy wrist and knee pads they rent right along with the skates and blades.

From the shops, it's a short walk on the asphalt path back to Lincoln Memorial Drive; turn right at the lagoon and head back to McKinley Beach.

"Like a gladsome creature in first panlette, young Milwaukee has gone with a hop, skip, and jump . . . being composed of representatives from all the migratory nations upon the earth, and especially from the universal Yankee."
Milwaukee Sentinel and Gazette, *July 26, 1847*

No. 7 Bay View Walk

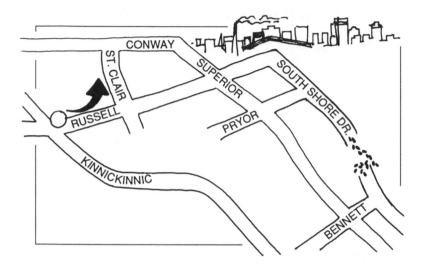

Distance
3.3 miles

How to Begin
I-794 over the Hoan Bridge drops you at Lincoln Memorial Drive.
Travel south on Lincoln Memorial to Russell Street. Drive west on
Russell to the corner of Russell and Kinnickinnic Streets.

Introduction
The village of Bay View was incorporated in 1879 and an-
nexed by Milwaukee in 1887. It was a true melting pot with
the original Yankee settlers arriving in the 1830s, the Germans
in the 1840s, and the iron laborers from the British Isles in the
1860s and 1870s.

In 1834, Horace Chase, Samuel Brown, and Morgan L. Burdick came by land from the Chicago Trading Post, traveling for four days from Chicago to Bay View. At that time, Juneautown, Kilbourntown, and Walker's Point had already been established.

Bay View's development as an industrial suburb began when Eber Brock Ward from Detroit established the Milwaukee Iron Company in 1867 to manufacture Bessemer steel. After Ward died, the company reorganized as North Chicago Rolling Mills, and in 1889, it became Illinois Steel Company. The iron mills needed workers and many Bay View homes were built for them, which may account for the unusual number of modest homes overlooking Lake Michigan on Shore Drive and Superior Street.

Now, Bay View is a middle-class neighborhood where most of the homes were renovated in the 1970s and 1980s. Their charm confirms the importance of maintaining Milwaukee's neighborhood heritage.

It's hard to say it without stumbling. Most people emphasize the first "K" and say "Kinnic" twice. That's easy, and it's where **this walk starts at the intersection of Kinnickinnic and Russell Streets.**

The Church of the Immaculate Conception dominates this corner. In 1907, the new church's name represented a victory for the ladies. The men wanted to name it after Saint Patrick and the women wanted to honor the Immaculate Conception, so to settle the issue, votes were sold, with the proceeds going to the building fund. The ladies won.

Walk east from here on Russell and notice the "painted lady" at 1054. Take a break at Bits of Britain. For fifteen years this small shop has supplied Milwaukee with British imports while retaining an authentic character. Its location, obscure at best, draws visitors by word of mouth and a lot of people must be talking because it's thriving. This is Milwaukee's only British import shop.

Come from 11:00 a.m. – 3:00 p.m. for teatime and delight in a traditional "cream tea": scones, Devon cream, and a pot of English tea. There are just five tables, each covered with a lace tablecloth.

Farther down Russell, turn left on St. Clair and you can go directly from teatime to dinner in the midst of Old World charm at Three Brothers Bar & Restaurant, located in a building constructed in 1897 for the Schlitz Brewing Company. Today, owner Branko Radicevich uses only traditional family recipes and his *burek* is considered one of the finest around. If the food here is good enough for famed French chef Julia Child, it must be pretty good Serbian chow. When Child visited Milwaukee in 1990, she dined at Three Brothers because her press agent wanted her "to see not only the city's fancy spots but good homecooking restaurants as well."

Follow Conway around the corner and keep bearing right until it becomes Superior Street. Here's the main artery of Bay View and a street that showcases the astounding number of homes that have been renovated. You'll see "painted ladies" at 2522, 2577, and at 2590, where Bay View's first lending library was established in this residence belonging to Beulah Brinton, a social activist ahead of her time. In 1924, when she was almost ninety, the Beulah Brinton Community House was opened in her honor.

Just around the corner on Pryor is Milwaukee's last public artesian well, the Pryor Avenue Iron Well where people can supply themselves with iron-rich waters drawn from deep under the city. **Turn right on Pryor to find the well.**

Two blocks south at 2739 Superior Street, a little white church built in 1868 has served three denominations in 122 years. It began as a Congregational church, in 1908 passed to Lutheran ownership, and in the 1940s became a Christian Scientist chapel. It would have been quite at home in the television version of "Little House on the Prairie"; it is very unlike the dominant churches on Milwaukee's South Side.

Turn toward Lake Michigan on Bennett Street and when you come to Shore Drive, walk south to the end, then turn around and follow Shore back to Russell.

These homes on Shore have the best view in Milwaukee. People who live here can glance out a front window and see the city's skyline, the harbor, and to the east, open water and a parade of incoming and outgoing ships. The best of the best must be sunrise seen from the screened porch at 3019 Shore. Farther down the road at 2582, a white frame house built around 1870 rivals the grandeur of North Shore mansions, for both its design and setting possess nineteenth century grace and charm.

If there seem to be many sailboats on the lake along here, it's because the South Shore Yacht Club, founded in 1910, is located at Nock Street. Just south of the club, South Shore Park, originally a farm, offers a stunning view of the bay, a nice sandy beach, and a kiddie playground. At the corner of Estes and Shore, notice the knarled beech tree straight out of *The Hobbit*.

Turn left on Russell and follow it back to Kinnickinnic and if you're hungry, drop into G. Groppi's Italian Grocery Store, established in 1913, for some of their fresh cannoli.

"Bay View has the majesty of the lake at its door-step. More than anything else, the lake gives the neighborhood a serenity, a sense of relationship with the world beyond the human. Not surprisingly, many Bay Viewites develop what amounts to a spritual relationship with Lake Michigan."

Bay View Wisconsin, John Gurda, 1979

"One of Bay View's favorite myths is that you have to know someone to buy a house there. According to popular legend, houses are treated like family jewels, and they are passed down only to relatives and close friends."

Bay View Wisconsin, John Gurda, 1979

"The rolling mill gave birth to the village of Bay View, and it was a major local institution for more than sixty years. Hundreds of Bay Viewites set their clocks by the mill whistle and they watched every night when the molten slag was poured into the lake and lit up the sky like the Fourth of July."

Bay View Wisconsin, John Gurda, 1979

No. 8 Historic Walk

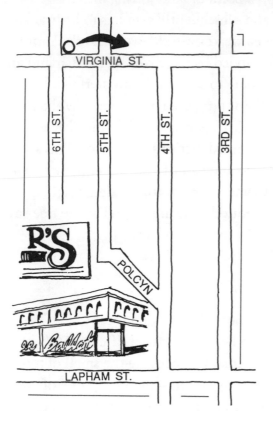

Distance
2.0 miles

How to Begin
Take the National Avenue exit off I-94 just south of downtown. Travel east on National to 6th Street, turn north, drive to Virginia Street, and park at the corner of 6th and Virginia.

Introduction
Downriver from the land Solomon Juneau and Byron Kilbourn claimed, George H. Walker, number three in the trio of Mil-

waukee founders, staked his claim. In 1834, he built a cabin and a trading post on a point of land jutting into the Menomonee River and subsequently sold lots to Milwaukee's early citizens. The area we know today as Walker's Point was heavily wooded, surrounded by riverbank and marshland and in the summertime, home to thousands of waterfowl. Despite a slow start, Walker's Point prospered and George Walker went on to become mayor of Milwaukee and the Point became one of the most ethnically mixed sections of the city. This small area north of Greenfield and east of 16th street became a forest of church steeples. Come along on this modest neighborhood walk and leave the twentieth century behind at the freeway entrance at National Avenue. Step backwards in time into historic Milwaukee.

Y ou can't avoid awareness of history on these streets. **A good place to begin is in front of Conejito's at the corner of 6th and Virginia.** Chances are the smell of tortillas cooking will remind you to stop in sometime at one of Milwaukee's least pretentious restaurants where Mexican gourmands consistently return to devour tasty guacamole and hot, hot salsa.

Walk east on Virginia to 4th Street and take a short half- block detour to Holy Trinity Roman Catholic Church. It sits on land purchased from George Walker and was built by German-speaking Catholics living on the South Side who contributed lumber, bricks, love, and labor to make this magnificent building, dedicated in 1850.

That's fifty-six years before the first Milwaukee Trade School opened. After it burned in 1909, the building at 319 Virginia replaced the original School of Trades. Turn **right around the corner by the school on 3rd Street,** where a block of vintage homes built in the mid-1800s looks like a parade of homes designed to showcase Milwaukee Cream City brick.

It's pretty special, this brick that's responsible for Milwaukee being known to this day as the "Cream City." In 1835, the first Cream City brickyard began operating, and from there a huge industry evolved. By the 1850s, eight local brickyards employed more workers than the breweries. Milwaukee sits on clay left over from the last Ice Age and the builders used it to produce bricks. Thanks to unusually large percentages of calcium and magnesium in the clay, the bricks turn pale yellow when they are fired—thus, the nickname, Cream City. Use of this brick declined in the early 1900s when soot from industry obscured its subtle color.

A number of houses in the 600 and 800 blocks on 3rd Street have been renovated and the original Cream City brick has been exposed. Notice the penthouse rooms on the rooftops of 634 and 640. What views they have! These homes were built for a lake captain and a foundry owner.

At Washington Street, the Guadalupe Center houses a variety of educational and recreational programs. The building was designed for the Wisconsin Telephone Company in 1899. From here look up to a skyscape dominated by the 280-foot-tall Allen-Bradley clock tower. This landmark, completed in 1963, serves as an official navigation aid on Coast Guard maps and an unofficial aid for the rest of us who don't wear a watch but occasionally need to know the time. This lighted, four-sided clock tower is the largest of its kind in the world.

Look closely at the home at 1137 Third Street. Such a hodgepodge of styles could only have been added in chunks and layers at different times. It looks like the snail's home in Leo Lionni's children's book, *The Biggest House in the World*.

At Lapham Street turn right, then turn right again at 4th Street and angle left onto Polcyn Street as it parallels I-94.

Here, St. Stephen's Evangelical Lutheran Church is in Gothic revival design and unusually ornamented for this period. Like the cathedrals of the Middle Ages, perhaps its complexity is the reason why it took fifty-plus years to build. The stained glass windows alone must have taken many years to design and execute.

Follow Polcyn Street until it turns into 5th Street and enter the commercial heart of Walker's Point. At 734, members of Walker's Point Development Corporation work diligently to preserve the historic character of the neighborhood.

At 5th and National Avenue the former Tivoli Palm Garden houses the Milwaukee Ballet Company. Above the entrance, the Schlitz trademark tells of its past as an outdoor beer garden and an indoor palm garden. Large murals provided a romantic background of palm trees and opulent sunsets for evenings filled with laughter, music, and beer.

National Avenue was once the area's main commercial street and it still draws customers looking for Mexican groceries and restaurants. Just past the Garden on 5th, the Super Mercado Trejo supplies the neighborhood and beyond with supermarket ingredients for Mexican meals. No one should leave here without the makings of a home-cooked Mexican feast. It smells so good, and everything on the shelves is inviting and mysterious. You know all you need is a recipe and some time, and anything is possible. Come early and snack on warm tortillerias from El Rey Mexican Products down the street.

Turn left onto Virginia to find Conejito's and the end of this historic Walker's Point walk.

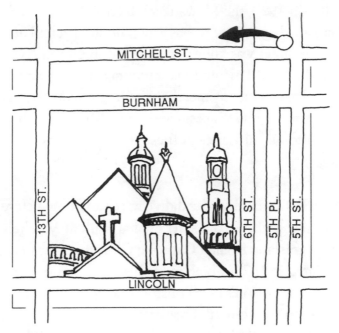

Distance
2.5 miles

How to Begin

Just south of Milwaukee on I-94, follow the freeway signs to Mitchell Street, and park near the corner of Mitchell and 5th Streets.

Introduction

Mitchell Street was established in the mid-1800s when Alexander Mitchell donated money for a street to connect Walker's Point in the east with the Janesville Plank Road (now Forest Home Avenue). Now it's hard to picture Mitchell and Lincoln Streets the way they were when they were new and fresh and filled with the hopes and dreams of the Polish immigrants who settled there in the 1860s. Back then, these tree-lined thoroughfares filled with pedestrians and trolleys served up a menu of merchants who sold residents everything they needed. In 1920, the Milwaukee Electric Railway and Light Company began a motorbus route along Mitchell and in the 1930s, the street was known as the "Polish Grand Avenue." Today, Mitchell and Lincoln look discouraged. Many changes have taken place and many merchant entrepreneurs have come and gone in the seventy years since the neighborhood's heyday, but the historical significance of these streets remains.

*T*hose early Polish immigrants didn't waste any time before establishing a church. **At the start of this walk at Mitchell and 5th, is St. Stanislaus Roman Catholic Church,** organized in 1886, dedicated in 1873, which made history when its parishioners founded the nation's first Polish-speaking elementary school. Between the church's organization and the dedication, members mortgaged their homes and their lives to build it. Look upward at the golden domes of this Renaissance- style church. Those twin peaks represent God and Country. They used to be copper, but in 1962, they were coated with genuine gold.

From this impressive start, **travel west on Mitchell to 13th Street** and the Farm Market. Along the way you'll pass shops, restaurants, and other services. Ethnic food selections include Middle Eastern at Sinbad's and the Casablanca, Greek at the Athens Family Restaurant, and Nicaraguan food at Taqueria La Carreta Nica. Don't let the unassuming surroundings at La Carreta Nica send you past creative cooks Ramon and Candida Barbarena who serve up authentic dishes such as a nacatamele plate and tacos a la nica. Their green hot sauce isn't too hot and you can wash it all down with a glass of "tamarind" juice.

This juice from the tamarind fruit won't taste anything like a familiar fruit from the local greengrocer. They make it by boiling something that looks like a banana for an hour. After the pulp has been strained, chilled, and poured over ice, the taste is superb.

Down the block, when you step into Goldmann and Sons, established in 1896, a time warp beams you back to the dry goods stores of the 1950s. Remember cotton dusters and girdles? Those girdles are best forgotten—especially the ones with dangling garters (to hold up seamed nylons) and elastic so skintight that it just stretched enough to let you in and then squeezed your extra inches from below to above. Goldmann's, crammed full of memories, still maintains its well-deserved reputation for the best bargains in town.

The next attraction on Mitchell is "Bridal Row," where seven shops in two blocks compete for the same customers. Just beyond at 13th Street, the Farm Market sits in the place where St. Jacobi Church fell to the wrecking ball in 1977. It must have been a sad day when this massive brick and stone structure crumbled and dropped to the street.

Turn south here and follow 13th to Lincoln. Thirteenth could use a facelift, perhaps cosmetic surgery. There are a number of interesting homes along here that date back to the late 1800s: 1824-26, a Cream City brick store and residence; 1924-24A, a Polish flat; 1949, an example of two homes built by Polish immigrants on the same lot; 1966, fabricated to look like split stone and accented with a tooled mortar line; and finally, 2051 and 2063, two Cream City brick homes.

At Lincoln, turn left and walk back to 5th Street. Do you need a passport photo, bar supplies, beauty aids, bait, a television set, a funeral, or dentures? This is the place! Is your toaster, shoe, couch, watch, alternator, or awning in disrepair? Get it fixed here!

Along Lincoln you'll pass Kosciuszko Park, originally part of the estate of Universalist minister Clement F. Le Feure. The park was named in honor of General Thaddeus Kosciuszko of Revolutionary War fame, and embellished with an equestrian statue of the General sculpted in 1905 by Florentine Gaetano Trentavone. Funds for the monument were raised by neighborhood residents.

At 6th and Lincoln, the Basilica of St. Josephat represents Polish ingenuity and a backbreaking labor of love. Materials salvaged from the main post office in Chicago and transported to Milwaukee on five hundred railroad flatcars provided the materials for this magnificent house of worship. The builders knew how to recycle, and with their $20,000, they bought limestone and marble, polished granite columns, metalwork, and woodwork which was transformed into an awesome neo-Renaissance church. It is Milwaukee's largest church and it has one of the largest steel domes in the country.

Across the street, Old Town Restaurant has served excellent Serbian food for many years, and close by, La Hacienda serves up great, inexpensive Mexican fare. **From here turn back toward Mitchell and walk north on 5th Place to Burnham.**

Fifth Place has its own unique personality. When eighteen homes line a single block, each with a different roofline and front porch, each sitting just four feet from the sidewalk, it's easy to imagine how a tidy Polish working-class neighborhood must have looked one hundred years ago. Listen carefully and you may hear long-ago laughter in the streets and the chatter of the housewives as they watched their children. Look behind from Burnham to Lincoln and notice how the skyline is dominated by St. Josephat's. You can feel the community of those immigrants and their magnificent church.

Jog left on Burnham and right on 6th and return to Mitchell and the start of this South Side adventure.

No. 10   Third Ward Walk

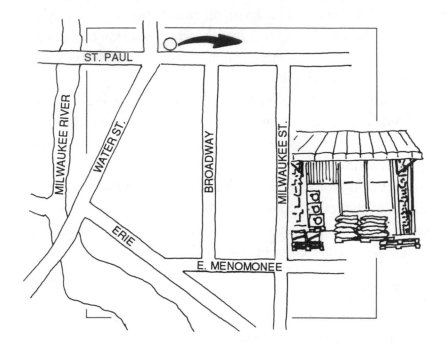

Distance
One mile

How to Begin
Take I-794 east and exit on Plankinton. This brings you to St. Paul
Avenue. Cross the river on St. Paul and park at the corner of St.
Paul and Water Street.

Introduction
Instead of a loop, this is a zigzag. The Historical Third Ward is
small, bordered by the Milwaukee River, St Paul Avenue, and
the freeway. It's rich in history. The first settlers were fur

traders and fishermen, and gradually, as Milwaukee settled, wholesale warehouses moved in. This happened after the railroad linked Milwaukee to the Mississippi River in 1856, and wholesalers were able to supply necessities to settlers in the west. Many Irish immigrant laborers who came to Milwaukee in the 1840s to escape the potato famines, lived in the Third Ward and supplied the manpower.

Tragedy struck in 1892 when a fire destroyed 440 buildings and left 1,900 people homeless. After the fire, immigrants from Italy moved into the neighborhood and established the grocery commission houses in the area known as Commission Row. After World War II, warehousing declined and the freeway displaced the Italian community. In the 1970s, renovation began, and by 1984, seventy-one buildings had been accepted by the National Register of Historic Places.

*H*ere's another view of downtown Milwaukee. **From the corner of Water and St Paul,** look north across the freeway past the construction to the skyline. Could anyone have imagined, back in the 1850s when the Third Ward community began, that freeways would replace rails, that semis on interstate highways would deliver produce to Commission Row, and that the Mississippi River would be less than a half-day's drive away?

The charm of the Third Ward is in the juxtaposition of history and technology. The past speaks in the buildings that remain from the reconstruction after the devastation in 1892. One of these is the former F. Mayer Boot and Shoe Company building from 1910. Today it houses the Milwaukee Institute of Art and Design and the Palette Shop, which carries a wide range of materials for artists. It's not too difficult to spot MIAD students on their way to class—their funky clothes and interesting hairdos are out of the ordinary. On the lower level of the building, the Palette Shop overflows with raw materials of creativity and books that makes art look as easy as ABC.

Walk east on St. Paul to the Third Ward Caffe where quattro formaggio (tricolor pasta in a sauce of four cheeses) sounds good for lunch, or you can have squid steak sauteed with onions, black olives, and tomatoes for dinner. They call it calamari roma. The Caffe is located in one of the few buildings that survived the 1892 fire. Constructed in 1875, it was originally the home of Jewett and Sherman Company, preparers of coffee and spices.

At the next corner, business is over by 10 a.m. and the barricade of trucks has moved on. By mid-morning on Commission Row, unloading is finished and the produce has been sent off to local markets. This was the heart of the Italian neighborhood and Milwaukee's fresh fruit and vegetable market still thrives there today. Come early and you might see a moving van-size truck filled with watermelons, or a cube of Sno-Bunny lettuce boxes from California that measures six feet by six feet by six feet. Is that a lot of lettuce? Could be 10,000 heads, right there on their way to market.

Turn right at Milwaukee Street, and if you love hunting for antiques, don't walk past the Milwaukee Antique Center at the corner where three floors and 75 dealers serve both retail customers and other dealers. The building used to be the home of O. H. Hansen Glove and Mitten Manufacturing Company.

Across the street, the Otto Kuehn Leaf Tobacco Warehouse holds the offices of Erv Julien Shade Company. Next door, at the Milwaukee Inn Restaurant a sign in the window appeals, "Eat here or we'll all starve." Close by is the Landmark Building at 316 North Milwaukee Street where Nance's has quickly established a reputation as one of Milwaukee's fine restaurants. She starts with a $3.95 hamburger and moves upscale to swordfish with lime pistachio butter at $17.95.

Turn right on East Menomonee Street past Catalano Square. You might wonder: how did a triangle became a square? **At the corner of Menomonee and Broadway turn right again** and you'll see the current home of Theater X in a building that used to be a grocery warehouse.

At 176 North Broadway, Engine Company Number 10 was established in 1893. This firehouse has the unusual distinction of being the only fire station in Milwaukee to be destroyed by fire! It has a beautiful red brick exterior with oak doors that display loving care given to a relic of Milwaukee's past.

For fun, drop in across the street at Broadway Paper where they sell bags, boxes, napkins, and fancy hat boxes both wholesale and retail. In the back room, Cream City Ribbon ships its products all over the country.

Walk a little farther and the aroma of freshly ground coffee will lure you into Northwestern Coffee Mills, where they import, roast, blend, and grind 45,000 pounds of coffee, tea, and spices each year. They roast the coffee beans on the spot. Unlike many distributors, they don't sell flavored beans because they believe the purity of the original flavor is compromised by adding extracts. They'll sell you a cup of freshly brewed coffee and on a balmy day you can sit outdoors at a table and watch the world walk past.

In the next block, the LoftSpace Building, the site of another wholesale grocery business, houses La Boulangerie, a popular cafe, as well as Eccola, Phoenix Design, the Private Gardener, and the Gingrass Gallery (see the Third Ward Art Walk).

In La Boulangerie, sunlight streams in while morning customers wake up sitting on fire engine-red chairs at old wood tables beneath exposed black and red ducts and pipes. There's no place like it for morning buns, real coffee, and good conversation.

Eccola features European imports. In their own words, "describing Eccola is almost impossible because of our unique point of view . . . many of our items are one of a kind while others pour out of the mold in great numbers." Here, "unique" is an understatement.

After LoftSpace, turn left on St Paul, left on Water, and follow Water past the Great Lakes Futon Company, dealers in kites and futons, and **walk all the way back to Erie Street and the Milwaukee River.**

You should have been at that corner the day Dillinger came to town, when television cameras turned it into a 1930s set, and dozens of extras in double-breasted, pin-striped suits milled around. Mark Harmon starred in this made-for-television movie in 1991.

You might be lucky enough to hear bells ring and see the Water Street Bridge separate and rise in midsection to let a tugboat and a barge chug past. You can charter a fishing boat here from Wally's Charter Service and follow the Milwaukee River under the Hoan Bridge into Lake Michigan.

To return, choose Milwaukee Street, Water Street, or Broadway and travel north back to the start.

> *"As early as 1856, the City Council had attempted to prevent citizens from throwing garbage in the streets, but it took police regulations in 1886 . . . to achieve the desired results, and even then it was deemed impossible to compel every housekeeper to keep a waste barrel as was done in some cities of the Union."*
>
> Daily Sentinel, *April 19, 1867*

No. 11 Third Ward Art Walk

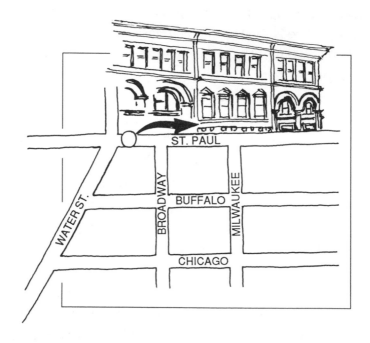

Distance
Eight short blocks

How to Begin
Take I-794 and exit on Plankinton Avenue, which will take you south to St. Paul Avenue. Cross the river at St. Paul and park at the corner of St. Paul and Water Streets.

Highlights
To read about the rest of the attractions in the Third Ward, see Walk No. 10. This walk will lead you to seven artist's galleries.

Start on the sixth floor of the Milwaukee Institute of Art and Design at the corner of Water and St. Paul where revolving shows include, of course, student art. At ground level, the Palette Shop sells supplies to artists, and dreams to the rest of us who fantasize about creating great art—some day.

Follow St. Paul east to Milwaukee Street, turn right and look for White Thunder Wolf Studio at the corner of Milwaukee and Buffalo Streets. It sells "handcrafted works of essence and feeling," including original art, jewelry, Native American crafts, unusual musical instruments, and tapes. Everything in the studio connects to Native American traditions. They have a drum collection, drum-making kits, drumming classes, and drum-making workshops. (They moved to 320 E. Clybourn Street in May 1992.)

Down the street at 233, the Tory Folliard Gallery, a 1990 newcomer, specializes in contemporary art. Inside, everything is white, designed to highlight the multifaceted personalities the gallery exhibits. The effect here is bright, colorful, gay, and lively. Revolving shows bring new talent several times a year.

Close by at 207 Milwaukee, the well-established Posner Gallery also displays a collage of contemporary art. Posner has been in business for twenty-six years, in this location for four, and an extensive collection of nineteenth and twentieth century art affirms the owner's competence in the art business.

It's well worth a trip to the gallery just to see the architecture. Two levels joined by a double staircase and a circular balcony halfway up give visitors a chance to pause and look over the art scene below. Seven thousand feet of grey carpeted space houses the gallery, a frame shop, and a wholesale catalog poster business that keeps a staff of eleven busy.

Posner's an expert on New Guinea art and once a year, usually in summertime, the gallery show will be devoted to recent acquisitions purchased in New Guinea. The rest of the year, revolving shows often spotlight Wisconsin artists.

From here, turn right on Chicago Street, again on Broadway, and let your nose follow the aroma of Northwestern Coffee Mills into 217, veer left past the grey and red wall of light into the Dean Jensen Gallery. This simple, uncluttered space invites contemplation of a variety of dramatic revolving shows.

A few doors north at 241 Broadway, Gingrass Gallery and the Private Gardener blend together in an unusual combination of twentieth century art and exotic plants. The Gingrass Gallery exhibits decorative art, jewelry, and crafts as well as fine art while the Private Gardener next door overflows with lush foliage in every imaginable shape and size. Together they make a provocative statement about sources of art, for it's hard to separate art from an underlying context of natural forces and forms.

Continue north to St. Paul, turn left and walk one block back to Water Street.

> "A correspondent at the mouth of the Milwauky, speaks of their having a town already laid out; of selling quarter acre lots for five and six hundred dollars, and says that by fall there will be one hundred buildings up . . . that some 50-100 people are living there . . . Land speculators are circumambulating it, and the Milwauky is all the rage."
>
> Green Bay Intelligencer and Wisconsin Democrat,
> *June 27, 1835*

No. 12 Downtown Gallery Walk

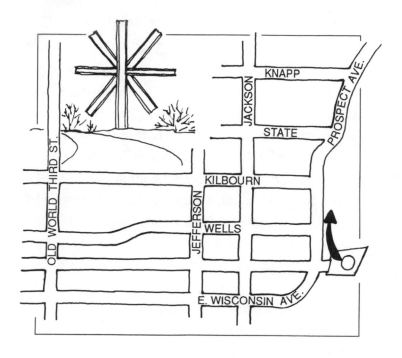

Distance
3.2 miles

How to Begin
Take I-794 east and exit at Lincoln Memorial Drive. Travel north on Lincoln Memorial to the Milwaukee Art Museum, an appropriate start for this art walk.

Introduction
Though downtown Milwaukee can't rival New York's gallery scene, a growing number of local galleries consistently exhibit

an exciting selection of classic and contemporary art. From the Milwaukee Art Museum's developing collection to the funky A. Houberbocken, Inc., these downtown galleries affirm art is alive and thriving in Milwaukee.

Start this walk from the rooftop plaza of the Art Museum. Take a few minutes here to ponder age-old questions regarding the existence of art, exactly what it is or isn't, and be sure to notice the sculptures along the lakefront. If you're there on a school day, it's likely that the art will be covered with climbing and sliding children. To them, these priceless sculptures are just playground equipment.

Before you leave the plaza, take a careful look at the city skyline. There's art, silhouetted against the sky, and it's free. Even a common construction crane, sign of progress and change, forms a striking linear pattern against a clear blue backdrop.

Two observations expressed by children walking away from the Museum's outdoor sculpture garden: "It gives me a feeling I never felt before" and "Looks like a couple of rocks stuck together." Both speak to the unique perspective each of us brings to art.

The entrance fee at the Art Museum is $4.00 for adults, $2.00 for students and seniors, and free to members and children under twelve.

Walk north on Prospect Avenue along Juneau Park past a statue of Solomon Juneau, larger than life, holding an oar and looking appropriately solemn. Mr. Juneau was both our first white settler and Milwaukee's first mayor.

At the corner of State Street and Prospect Avenue, the David Barnett Gallery is located in a grand old Cream City brick building. Ring the bell to enter the elegant setting for an extensive array of art. Owner David Barnett has been in the business for twenty-five years and his collection shows his experience and good taste. Upstairs are several rooms filled with paintings and sculpture and downstairs more art and a frame shop.

David Barnett has a permanent collection as well as several revolving shows each year. As you walk through the gallery, watch for Susan Falkman's marble sculptures. Barnett handles Falkman's work locally and her marble pieces are particularly expressive.

The home for this gallery cost $30,000 when it was built in 1875 for Dr. Henry Harrison Button—an extravagant price in those days. Its nine thousand square feet houses eight fireplaces, hardwood floors and twelve-foot ceilings. Built in an Italianate substyle of Victorian architecture, the house has a spectacular asymmetrical plan, exterior walls of Cream City brick, and a considerable amount of handmade ornamentation. That's an unusual combination of features for a twentieth century gallery.

After leaving the Barnett Gallery, follow Prospect to Knapp Street and turn left. At 1119 East Knapp, the recently opened (1989) Peltz Gallery shows contemporary art, again in an historic setting. Owner Cissie Peltz has renovated another late nineteenth century Victorian home and converted it to a space where she can show off an eclectic collection that includes many Wisconsin artists as well as nationally known figures such as Oldenburg, Pearlstein, and Cristo. Many of the artists shown at the Peltz Gallery base their work in realism.

At the corner of Marshall and Knapp, you'll pass the Lincoln Center for the Arts. Local artists and performers rent space here, including Friends Mime Theater, Jump Dance Theater, and Susan Falkman from the Barnett Gallery.

Stay on Knapp, walk through a parking lot, and you'll

come out on Jackson. Turn left to find the Larson Gallery, Ltd., at the corner of Jackson and Wells. This sleek contemporary gallery, done in grey with black and chrome furniture, displays a variety of posters and late model art. Prices range from $20 earrings to a $5,000 serigraph.

From here, angle through Cathedral Square Park and walk west on Kilbourn. At the southeast corner of Kilbourn and Broadway, the wall of Old St. Mary's Catholic Church is a good place to sit, surrounded by an exhilarating landscape. Architectural styles, lines, colors, shapes, and reflections comingle to form a cohesive urban portrait of downtown Milwaukee.

Next turn left on Old World Third Street and walk one block and turn left on Wells. Tucked into the second floor of the Century Building above Radio Doctors is A. Houberbocken, Inc. This tongue-twister comes from the names of the four owners—Houlehen, Berghauer, Bock, and Kennedy. This gallery is fun and a good place to find an artsy gift at a reasonable price. Their shows have unusual themes, such as teapots, the circus, clay vessels, and furniture.

Art galleries come and go and even though I've included many in the three Art Walks in this book, some of them will move on in the next few years. Because of the areas chosen for the Art Walks, the ones that leave very likely will be replaced by other galleries and interesting shops. For example, the Artisan Trade Gallery, formerly located at 137 Wells, opened in February 1990 and closed in January 1991.

At the corner of Wells and Jefferson, William De Lind Fine Art looks inviting, with Dennis Pearson's "beasties" peering out the window. These fiberglass creatures painted in cheerful colors draw visitors into this friendly gallery. William De Lind describes the selection in his gallery as simply "me." His art is fun.

His answer confirms that the personalities of gallery collections represent the owner's personal taste and preferences. Galleries differ, and this makes an interesting art walk.

Walk south on Jefferson to Wisconsin, turn left on Wisconsin, and head straight back to the Art Museum. The final object of contemplation will be *The Calling*, the controversial Di Suvero sculpture at the end of Wisconsin Avenue. Are these leftover sections from a freeway bridge glued together like a giant tinker toy? Did the artist play a joke on the trusting citizens of Milwaukee, or is it "art"?

"One of the wonders of the nineteenth century is the growth of American cities. Twenty-eight years ago, Milwaukee was a small, unimportant village, situated on two bluffs and divided by a sluggish river and an almost impenetrable tamarack swamp. Now on the same grounds stands . . . the home of a hundred thousand busy people and in the midst of the whilom tamarack swamp . . . the most luxurious hotel west of New York."

Milwaukee Daily Sentinel, *February 3, 1869*

No. 13 Tree Walk

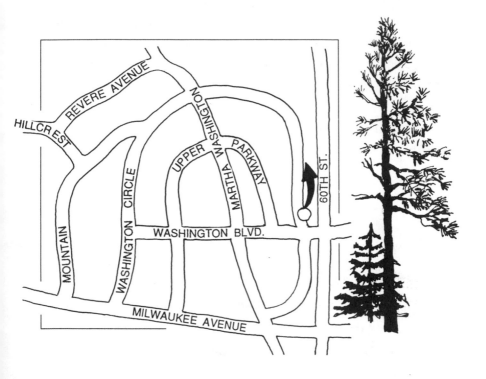

Distance
2.7 miles

How to Begin
Exit on 68th Street from I-94 west and travel north on 68th Street
to Milwaukee Avenue. Turn right on Milwaukee and left on 60th.
Enter Washington Highlands at the stop sign at Washington Boulevard.

Introduction
This walk is about trees. Some were planted and some grew
naturally in this part of Wauwatosa called Washington High-

lands. The Highlands has an interesting history. It was declared an historical landmark in 1978, for it's one of this country's earliest planned subdivisions.

In 1849, to start at the beginning, Hiram Ross bought 160 acres from the government. In 1865, he sold 180 acres to Thomas Brown for $17,000. Nice work! In the late 1800s, Pabst Brewery bought the land, and used it as a hops farm. In 1919, the heirs of the Pabsts incorporated the property, set up a board of directors to manage it, and laid down a set of rules to preserve the country feeling of the land. When the Highlands were set out, the Pabst family imported an architect from Germany, and rumor suggests that the main winding road resembles the shape of a Prussian helmet in honor of the German Kaiser.

Today, this is an area of rolling hills and terraces, trees and streams, bounded on the north and south by Lloyd Street and Milwaukee Avenue, and on the east and west by 60th and 68th Streets.

Someone once remarked that life is full of mixed blessings, except for trees. The Highlands is filled with trees. Old trees, dignified trees, trees that add character to this already dignified neighborhood. Annie Dillard writes in *Pilgrim at Tinker Creek*:

> Every year a given tree creates absolutely from scratch ninety-nine percent of its living parts. Water lifting up tree trunks can climb one hundred-fifty feet an hour; in full summer a tree can, and does, heave a ton of water every day. A big elm in a single season might make as many as six million leaves, wholly intricate, without budging an inch. . . . A tree stands there, accumulating dead wood, mute and rigid as an obelisk, but secretly it

seethes; it splits, sucks and stretches; it heaves up tons and hurls them out in a green, fringed fling . . . the dynamo in the tulip tree pumps out even more tulip trees, and it runs on rain and air.

Who can deny the magic of these giants among us? **At the corner of Washington Circle and Washington Boulevard where you entered the Highlands, turn right and follow Washington Circle to Martha Washington.** Here you'll enter a place that looks and feels just like an arboretum. In fact, the whole 2.7 miles will seem like a planned tree community. There's little traffic, the roads don't go anywhere, and at 6216 Washington Circle, the locust dressed in spring blossoms is a show-stopper.

Observe the number of lannon stone homes here. This stone comes from bedrock underneath clay deposited during the last Ice Age. This magnesium-rich limestone called Niagara dolomite was laid down as sediment in the bottom of the sea that covered this region more than three hundred million years ago. By the mid-1800s, quarries were removing the stone, and eventually a small village called Lannon in Waukesha County became a major supplier of what became known as "lannon stone." It was widely used in many subdivisions as well as by the WPA crews in Milwaukee County parks. There are many fine examples of lannon stone homes in the Highlands.

Back to the trees, **turn right on Martha Washington** and look for a large American linden, commonly known as basswood. It's a few feet from the south side of the house at 2026, and about thirty feet from the sidewalk. When this tree with its large heartshaped leaves blossoms, the air is heavy with sweet perfume.

North of the driveway at the same address and east of the sidewalk is a white cedar tree. This mid-sized evergreen, a Wisconsin native, was used by the Indians as a potent source of vitamin C to prevent scurvy.

Angle left on Revere and notice the maple canopy that shades the street. Because of the way the bark furrows follow growth lines in these trees, it appears they must have been trimmed when they were young. The dense canopy is reminiscent of a time in recent history when a squirrel could travel from Milwaukee to Boston on this green airborne carpet.

You have to look carefully to find the ponderosa pine tree at the corner of Revere and Hillcrest at 6726 Revere. Notice the needles in groups of threes and don't be fooled by the small red pine close by with two needles in each bundle. The ponderosa can grow to be a 250-foot giant in the Pacific Northwest, but here in Milwaukee we call 100 feet a big one. This is an important lumber tree and a source of serious conflict in its home states in the west.

Turn left on Hillcrest and watch for a maple at 6715 that appears to defy the law of gravity. From the outward horizontal growth pattern of the branches, it seems impossible that they can support their own weight as well as hundreds of thousands of leaves. You have to see it!

Turn right on Mountain and look for a huge white ash in the front yard at 1840. Nearby at 1821, in front of a red brick house, sit two weird-looking trees with little crowns and big trunks. These are weeping mulberry trees, and when the berries ripen in July, birds and people compete for the fruit.

At 1732 Mountain watch for a four-stem clustered bitternut hickory and just down the street at 1665 don't miss the tamarack, sometimes known as a European Larch. It has cones and branches that sweep out almost to the sidewalk. In the fall, this deciduous conifer will turn golden and all its needles will fall to the ground. As you walk past, be sure to run your hand across the needles.

Farther down the block at 1630, two very large sugar maples form a dense canopy that blocks sunlight from reaching the soil, thus preventing the growth of a standard suburban grassy lawn. Sugar maples dominate forests in Wisconsin on sites called "mesic," which means neither very wet nor very dry. Now, finding the rest of the interesting trees on this walk is up to you.

To complete the Highlands loop(s), turn
left on Milwaukee,
left on Upper Parkway South,
right on Washington Boulevard,
right on Washington Circle,
right on Martha Washington Drive,
left on Upper Parkway North,
right on Washington Boulevard,
and right on Washington Circle back to the start.

Half the fun of this walk is going round and round the helmet and not getting lost. The rest of the fun is spending a hour or two wandering around a suburban arboretum playing tree detective.

"As in the proposal of electricity for street lighting, the discussion of electric trolleys aroused popular apprehensions regarding the use of the 'dangerous stuff' . . . Everybody would be killed, and Milwaukee be turned into a regular angel factory."
Evening Wisconsin, *April 3, 1886*

No. 14 Shorewood Nature Walk

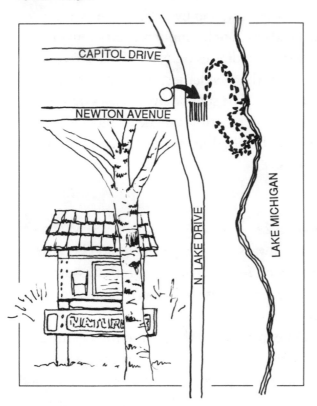

Distance
Half a city block

How to Begin
From I-43, take Capitol Drive east to North Lake Drive. Turn
south and watch for a sign announcing the Shorewood Nature
Preserve on the east side of the street at the corner of Newton
Avenue and Lake Drive. **Walk down the path to Lake Michigan.**

Introduction

In 1897, Shorewood incorporated as the Village of East Milwaukee. Its greatest attraction was a series of amusement parks on the east bank of the Milwaukee River. Starting in the 1920s, Shorewood grew rapidly, and by 1950, all the vacant land had been sold. Today, a single empty property remains nestled behind prominent addresses on North Lake Drive. It's easy to overlook this suburban wilderness. Even people who know it's there don't see it. The sign points to a woodchip path that leads down a bluff to a tiny secluded wild place. At the bottom, you'll find a beach, driftwood, and the swish of Lake Michigan's waves.

R obert Pirsig wrote in *Zen and the Art of Motorcycle Maintenance*, "In a car you're always in a compartment and because you're used to it, you don't realize that through that car window everything you see is just more TV. You're a passive observer."

This walk is about experiencing the great outdoors instead of watching it on television. It's about taking friends, family, children to a quiet place to explore, or to sit silently alone, and let the stillness pour through you. It's about Gandhi's observation, "There is more to life that increasing its speed." A place like the Shorewood Nature Preserve invites people to slow down.

Here there are endless seasonal events to note with a small celebration—maple sugaring, the first appearance of the pasque flower, the warbler's return, the grand opening of a spring pond, warm sand underfoot on the first summer day at the beach, golden aspen flickering under a blue sky in October, summer solstice, sunrises, sunsets, the list is long!

Edward Abbey wrote, "The best way to get to know this country, the only way, is with your body. On foot. Best of all, after scrambling to a high place, on your rump. Pick out a good spot and sit there, not moving for a year."

It's easier for country folks to do what Abbey suggests than for city dwellers who usually find their green spaces occupied with others' activities; however, there are times, even at a city hideaway like the Preserve, when private moments are available. Walk down at sunrise, or during off seasons like November and March or on a blustery winter storm day, and you're likely to find solitude.

City people have to try harder. So what if there are homes on the bluff above the Preserve and summer isn't the time for pristine silence? There's comfort in knowing this private walk exists.

"*The impression made upon strangers by the streets of a city has very much to do with its prosperity, with a favorable impression leading to an increase of population and capital. The value of real estate in a neighborhood depends much upon the cleanliness of the householders and the absence of unsightly ash barrels and slop buckets.*"
Milwaukee Sentinel, *April 25, 1886*

No. 15 Whitefish Bay Walk

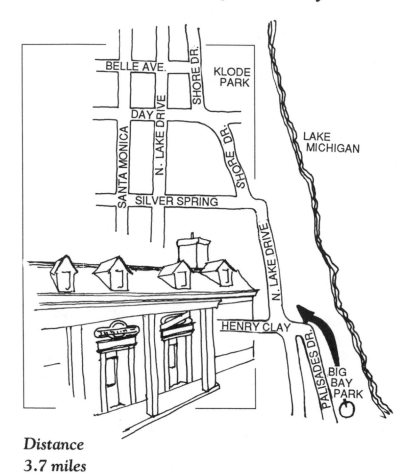

Distance
3.7 miles

How to Begin
Take the Hampton East exit off I-43 north and travel east on
Hampton Avenue to North Lake Drive. Two-tenths of a mile
north, where Lake Drive curves to the left, go straight on Palisades
Drive and park at Big Bay Park.

Introduction
This walk in the Village of Whitefish Bay will take you from

Big Bay Park along the Lake Michigan shoreline to Klode Park and back past the shops on Silver Spring Drive. This residential, or perhaps bedroom, community has some of the area's finest old homes. Young families regularly replace empty nesters here, as the good schools and sidewalks attract a flow of younger residents.

*B*ig Bay Park at the south end of Palisades Drive draws both families and lovers, for the romance of a sandy, secluded beach knows no limits. Those who fall under the spell of Lake Michigan will return again and again to witness the magic of a vast body of water. The concrete steps at the top lead to a beach below the wooded bluff where each spring the landscape at the bottom differs from previous years. Sometimes waves splash against the concrete walls, and other times the beach will be wide and inviting. An algae-encrusted concrete pier provides a place to settle down and watch waves disintegrate on the shore. Seldom crowded, this little park offers a small space for people who love Lake Michigan and like to encounter it from a solitary perspective.

From here, follow Palisades to Henry Clay and walk west to connect with Lake Drive again. Stop at 5270. Although Whitefish Bay became a village in 1892, it was still fairly primitive in 1919 when the Henry Uihleins moved into their huge house. They were the first to build in the Whitefish Bay subdivision and it must have been a little like camping out, with no paved roads, no sidewalks, and a mansion that ran on bottled gas.

This area, known as the Pabst subdivision, was an eighteen-acre parcel stretching north from Henry Clay along the narrow strip between the bluff and what's now Lake Drive. It began as the Pabst Whitefish Bay Resort, established in 1889 by Captain Frederick Pabst, and for twenty-five years, Milwaukeeans seeking a respite from the city made the five-mile trip by horse and carriage over the Lake Drive turnpike, by steamboat from the Grand Avenue dock in downtown Milwaukee, or by the trains which ran every forty-five minutes.

Patrons sipped beer at tables along the bluff or at a giant circular bar in the pavilion. Band music entertained them as they sipped, and later, a fashionable ferris wheel was installed. Many people were sad when the great resort closed in 1914.

The mansion at 5270 on the former site of the resort was occupied by the Uihleins from 1919 until 1946. In its heyday, every corner of the house was richly furnished. It included the most up-to-date technology— sixteen telephones, a central vacuum cleaning system, plate-warming cabinets in the butler's pantry, and a device that filtered rainwater for laundry were some of the innovative gadgets used by the Uihleins. A staff of ten servants ran the place. In 1953, a Roman Catholic order bought the house for $45,000. It is now privately owned. It's only one of the many spectacular homes along this section of Lake Drive that some call Milwaukee's "Gold Coast."

Around the bend, past the house with the red tile roof, turn right on North Shore Drive, go left on Day Avenue, right on North Shore Drive, and meander through the neighborhood to Klode Park. Come on a summer day and you won't find a better place to enjoy a lake breeze. Come when the sky is crystal blue and whitecaps march across the lake and everyone's happy. Whitefish Bay residents are proud of Klode Park. The recently constructed walk down the bluff to the lake followed a string of years when the lake threatened to reclaim the bluff and destroy the park. Now it's beautifully landscaped and it's a good place for a clear view of "whitefish" bay bounded by Fox Point and Shorewood.

Depart Klode Park on Belle Avenue, and turn left on Santa Monica Boulevard. Notice the elm trees. Villagers rose in a fury in the summer of 1990 when a poorly thought-out plan to "improve" Santa Monica included removing many of those priceless elms. Residents threw their bodies and parked their Mercedes automobiles against the trees to protest. The trees remained and the village eventually returned to normal.

At the corner of East Day Avenue, across the street from Richards School, a well-established wild yard obscures a small frame house. This little wilderness, a microcosm of Wisconsin woodlands, makes a green line for the homeowners and gives them serenity and privacy behind their tiny woodlot.

At Silver Spring, turn east to enjoy a wide variety of shops. "Must-sees" include Heinemann's Restaurant, where North Shore matrons mingle with shoppers and students; the Changing Scene, a good place to buy North Shore chic right off the rack; Harry W. Schwartz Bookshop, with bestsellers, classics, and off-beat books for adults on the ground floor and a sparkling collection for children on the lower level; the Bay Bakery, famous for their goods made with real butter; Sendiks, known for produce, deli, and grocery gossip; the Great Harvest Bread Company, where all the loaves are warm, and they insist you try a sample; and at the end of the street, Winkie's, the ultimate variety store.

Continue on Silver Spring and double back on Lake Drive to Big Bay Park. You'll pass Pandl's Whitefish Bay Inn at Woodburn Street and Lake Drive, and if it's time to eat, do stop in for a delicious German pancake.

No. 16 Beach Walk

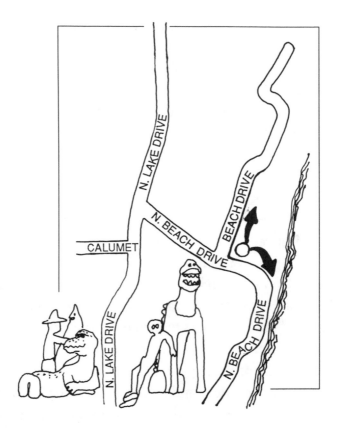

Distance
5.2 miles. (Six-tenths of a mile from the parking lot to Beach Drive; one mile to each end of the road.)

How to Begin
Take the Good Hope Road exit from I-43 north and travel north on Port Washington Road to Calumet Road. Turn east on Calumet and drive to Santa Monica Boulevard. Park in one of the church lots and **walk six-tenths of a mile east on Calumet, north on Lake Drive and down the hill on the Beach Drive footpath to the intersection where the walk officially begins.** From here

it's a mile in each direction to the end of the road. Don't be tempted to park in the street here—it's not allowed and tickets are given out freely.

Introduction

Hasty motorists on Lake Drive go right past the entrance to Beach Drive and the hill that slopes down to what is perhaps Milwaukee's most secluded neighborhood. Nestled between the beach and the bluff are houses that face the sunrise and sit at lake level. Walking along Lake Michigan on Beach Drive in Fox Point is enjoyable indeed.

*M*ultiple signs discourage curious motorists. "Permit parking only," "private driveway," "not a through road," "dead end," "turn here," "private road," "no turn around," and "trespassers prosecuted" suggest not-so-subtly that walkers leave their automobiles elsewhere. The message is clear.

Beach Drive is quiet. This walk doesn't include points of historical interest, great food, or commercial enterprises, but instead offers the tranquility that comes from being close to Lake Michigan and far away from crowded city beaches. Linger awhile and enjoy the lake while you peek unobtrusively into the yards of the people privileged to live on the beach.

You won't miss the auto traffic. Early in the morning and just before sunset, the birds get rowdy. Sometimes deer rustle leaves on the bluff. And on a windy day, when the gusts come from the east, Lake Michigan tosses noisy, boisterous waves on the shore.

Walk south and you'll come to a bend in the road and the incredible work of artist Mary Nohl. When Simon and Garfunkel wrote and recorded "The Sounds of Silence," could they have had 7328 Beach Drive in mind? Here's a yard, filled with strange figures that look as if someone planted them and they ripened into an art garden. They surround a small grey house tastefully decorated with classical low relief sculpture. Each colorful frieze set above outside windows and doors is different and many relate to the figures in the yard.

Those figures stand silently, watching Lake Michigan from behind a chain-link fence topped with rusty barbed wire. One seven-foot-tall figure has a rock head. Is this a reference to current hip slang for people who don't think because, in place of brains, they have a "box of rocks" on their shoulders? Remember the stick figures we drew in kindergarten? Here's one with a body made of half-inch-thick driftwood sticks. Even Leo Buscaglia wouldn't want to hug this one! One squeeze, and crunch—tinder for a fire. Most figures are concrete abstractions, half-beast, half-human, looking as if they're residents of a family whose bloodlines combine Matisse-like playfulness with Henry Moore's substantial humanity. Unlike museum sculpture gardens, touching is forbidden here. This is a private display.

From here walk south to the end of the road, then turn around and retrace your route to the intersection. To add two miles, walk north to the other end of the road and return to the parking lot the way you came.

No. 17 Wild Yard Walk

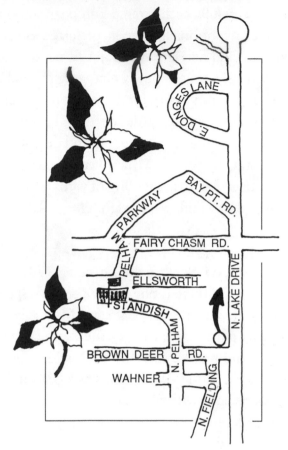

Distance
4.4 miles

How to Begin
Take the Brown Deer exit east from I-43 north and travel east to North Lake Drive. Park in George Pandl's Restaurant parking lot.

Introduction
Until recently, gardens were filled with exotics and hybrids—most of them imported from distant lands and crossbred for dependable blossoms. Traditionally, American gardeners have

ignored native plants and glorified English formal gardens instead. Native plants were removed and replaced by Kentucky bluegrass, carefully orchestrated European imports, and native hybrids. Conventional gardeners preferred masses of concentrated color and native plants don't fit neatly into that system.

Fortunately, time is slowly changing the public perception of a "garden." As concern for our environment increases and wilderness areas shrink, gardeners have begun to see native wildflowers and grasses as valuable and desirable. An exciting change is taking place in Milwaukee's landscape, and this walk will introduce you to a sampling of yards where homeowners have turned to wildflower gardening.

Walk north on North Lake Drive to 9701. Laurie Otto lives here and if there is one single person responsible for the return of native plants to the greater Milwaukee area, it's Laurie. Her advocacy, encouragement, and example have motivated most of the caretakers of "wild yards" around here.

Certainly, Laurie's yard stands as a beautiful example of what can be done with planning, hard work, and a great love for the land. She stopped mowing her lawn on the first Earth Day in 1970 and subsequently transformed it into something that closely resembles a native Wisconsin woodland. A white pine towers above her entrance and the needle path is soft— soft as it might have been when Indians walked here hundreds of years ago. Her acre is filled with native plants too numerous to mention. Laurie's personal favorite . . . the cup plant. In her words, "If I landed on a desert island and I could have only one plant, it would be a cup plant."

Why? "It's so architectural." This tall plant, with a square stem, golden flowers, and large leaves that hold pockets of water, attracts a seasonal procession of birds and butterflies.

Her wilderness includes Wisconsin woodland, a sand prairie, and a wetland that was formerly a roadside ditch. This glorious yard did not spring up in a season but required years of Laurie's careful attention to detail as she magically stole the land away from Kentucky bluegrass and restored it to something close to the original landscape.

Up the road to the north at the loop lies another wild yard. This one a prairie, grown from seed by homeowner Milt Ettenheim, showcases native plants and grasses all summer and into late fall. In June, his prairie explodes with blue baptisa and yellow buttercup.

From here, walk south on North Lake Drive to East Donges Lane and follow the loop in the shape of a horseshoe. In this wooded area are several examples of choices made by various homeowners to preserve their woods. Some cleared out the trees and planted bluegrass, some left small patches of woodland, and some left the area intact. There's a point here where grass replaces forest, and as you walk from one ecosystem into the other, notice the difference in light, temperature, shade and even humidity.

Continue to follow Lake Drive south. Turn west on Bay Point Road and south again on Pelham Parkway to 9256. Here's another wild yard, this one carefully landscaped, yet landscaped with native plants instead of hybrids and traditional cultivars. The impression is more like Monet's water lilies than Fragonard's gardens.

Jog left on Fairy Chasm and right to continue on Pelham Parkway. At Ellsworth Lane, turn right toward Bayside School and walk to the south end of the parking lot. Here grapevines, crabapple trees, and bittersweet mingle right outside classroom windows. This used to be a monoculture of crabapple trees surrounded by bluegrass and a chain link fence. Fifty children and five women from a local garden club, under the direction of Laurie Otto, worked in small groups to change the face of the area.

At a local landfill they dug asters, goldenrod, yarrow, and anything else that looked interesting; they bought bittersweet and raspberries from a garden center; from catalogs they ordered grapes, and small mountains of leaves were wheeled from a local dump. It was quite an undertaking.

Leave the school on Standish Place, walk east to Pelham Parkway, continue south on Pelham, east again on Wahner Road to North Fielding Road, and south to 8635. At last, here's a field on Fielding! In this yard, the owner plugged native plants into an existing lawn. This can be a slow process but when you see the yard, it's clear the results are well worth the effort.

From here, walk back on Fielding to Lake Drive and Pandl's, where the food is delicious and the Sunday brunch superb!

(To learn more about natural landscaping, contact the Schlitz Audubon Center, where each month a group called "The Wild Ones" meets to share resources and ideas. In the spring, members of this group grab their shovels and head for "bulldozer alerts" when plants need to be rescued at sites about to be excavated for new construction.)

"Criticizing Milwaukee is a favorite Milwaukee pastime . . . Milwaukeeans feel comfortable about their town. They don't need to brag about it. The old girl may be dull and somewhat dowdy, but she makes great Sauerbraten and she has Gemutlichkeit."
This Is Milwaukee, Robert W. Wells, 1970

No. 18 Garden Walk

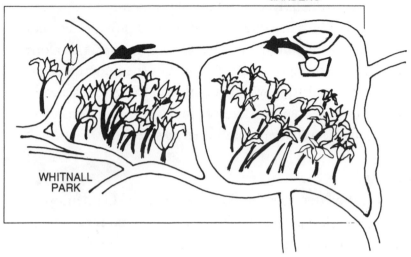

BOERNER
BOTANICAL
GARDENS

WHITNALL
PARK

Distance
2.2 miles

How to Begin
Whitnall Park and the Boerner Botanical Gardens are located off South 92nd Street in Hales Corners. To find the starting point for this walk, take I-894/I-43 and watch for signs directing motorists to the Gardens. There is a small fee to park in the lot on weekends, holidays, and for special events.

Introduction
Boerner Botanical Gardens, within Whitnall Park, display trees, shrubs and formal gardens in an open-air museum. The beginnings of the park and gardens date back to the early

1920s when Charles B. Whitnall convinced the County Board and the Park Commission to set aside land for a park in southwestern Milwaukee. While Mr. Whitnall was primarily responsible for land purchases, Alfred L. Boerner, then county landscape architect, was a powerful force in the development of the park and, particularly, the Botanical Gardens.

Mr. Boerner's belief that a park should provide aesthetic pleasure is evident in the combination of formal and informal plantings in the gardens. He believed in the importance of continuing education within a park and the gardens clearly offer unlimited combinations of plantings where homeowners can learn directly from professional gardeners.

Today, the Friends of the Boerner Botanical Gardens work with the staff in providing a wide variety of both indoor and outdoor programs for adults. In addition, the Friends established a children's horticulture program that serves thousands of youngsters each year.

Even the Garden House is unusual. The design carries out an "old Wisconsin farmhouse" theme with hand-hewn oak beams, a carved mantel, a native limestone fireplace, and an oak parquet floor. The stone exterior, composed of boulders hand-cut by WPA workers, came from moraines deposited by the same glacial action that formed Lake Michigan and the hills surrounding it.

The building was dedicated in 1939; however, work on the gardens dates back to 1932. From 1934-41 extensive planting was accomplished. The flowering crab apple collection and the lilac collection were early additions to the landscape. The crabapples were planted as part of the overall landscape plan after the park lagoons were completed in 1933. The lilacs were planted from 1937-1940, the tulip collection came in 1955, the rock garden in 1941, and the dwarf fruit trees in 1957.

The popular herb garden was begun in 1952, and today its collection of aromatic, culinary, and medicinal plants draws thousands of visitors each season.

This garden walk, a spring walk, barely touches the tip of a season here that extends from April through October for, in addition to the permanent collections, more than 25,000 annuals are planted each year. Here's a treasury of formal and informal gardens just south and west of Milwaukee.

Impressionist painter Edgar Degas dressed his ballerinas in pink. Perhaps in his travels in France he found a place like Whitnall Park, where each May, a showcase display of 1,100 pink flowering crabapple trees decorates grassy fields alongside the road that winds through the park.

Pink is an understatement. This flowering crabapple collection may be the most extensive and spectacular grouping in the country and without a doubt, they're the crown jewels of Whitnall Park and the Botanical Gardens while they are in full bloom.

May is a good time to visit. To see this pink explosion, come in mid to late May for timing is critical, and once displayed, the little blossoms soon blow away.

The best way to see the park and gardens is on foot. **Walk west from the Garden House and follow a 2.2 mile circle tour around Whitnall Park. At the first fork in the road, bear right. At the next intersection, follow the "76" bike sign to the left and from there turn left at each road crossing until the road loops back to the Garden House.**

After the circle tour, there's plenty more to see and do at the gardens. You could begin with the tulip collection across the road, where 21,000 tulips are massed in a display area surrounding a Dutch windmill. Unlike the ladylike crabapple trees, flamboyant tulips proudly exhibit themselves in April and May. This palette of primary colors consistently evokes "oohs" and "ahhs" from visitors as camera shutters click on every sunny day. It's hard to beat the simple beauty of a backlit red and yellow striped tulip carefully arranged on top of a perfectly round stem.

These tulips come at the end of a procession of spring bulbs that began with daffodils and narcissi. There's a Greek legend about the narcissus which tells of a beautiful young man by that name who was loved by a nymph called Echo. He didn't love her in return so she ceased to eat, faded away, and Narcissus was justly punished by the gods. One day, he bent over a pool, saw his face reflected in the water, and fell deeply in love with his own reflection. Poor Narcissus. He returned daily to admire himself and finally the pain of unrequited love led him to stop eating and he, too, faded away from lack of love. When the nymphs came to take his body, in its place was the white flower known as narcissus. In the cup, in the center of the blossom, were Echo's tears! Are they still there? Sometimes a little magic adds to the wonder of a beautiful place.

Visitors can create their own magic across the boardwalk in the bog garden. Talk should be banned here when people come to this lush green carpeted wetland. Not everyone will be willing to tiptoe in silence from end to end, but those who try will be rewarded with a serenade of spring birds and the peace that comes from human silence in a natural area.

In mid-May, yellow marsh marigolds highlight this green rug and young leaves begin to surround decaying skunk cabbage hoods where insect pollinators have already finished their spring chores.

By late May, much of the work is finished in the "pulpits." This wetland plant, known as "Jack in the pulpit," traps innocent flies and holds them inside until their pollination duties are complete before releasing them. For country kids, "Jack" provided great entertainment when they deviously initiated "city slickers" with a small edible sample of this plant. From a first mild bite, the taste becomes increasingly hot until it burns the mouth, tongue, and lips for several hours. Jack can be seen from the bridge over the bog.

The last hurrah of spring at the gardens happens when the peonies burst into their full chorale of pink and red glory with both single and double blossoms. This ostentatious display dispels rumors that "when you've seen one peony, you've seen them all."

What could be more romantic than a stroll through a spring garden?

"On the eve of its development, Milwaukee had a few drawbacks. Its rivers were still worthless for lake commerce. Much of its future downtown district was a bog, suitable only for ducks and mosquitos. At a time when the population was hardly sufficient for one village, three settlements had grown up, each hoping the other two would disappear. If Juneau, Kilbourn, and Walker had hired an urban planner to advise them, he would have certainly told them that this was no place to found a mighty city."
This Is Milwaukee, Robert W. Wells, 1970

No. 19 South Shore Lakefront Walk

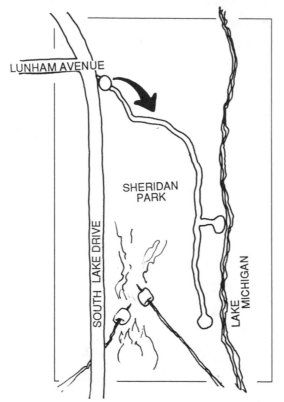

Distance
2 miles

How to Begin
From I-94 South, take Layton Avenue east to South Lake Drive, turn north and park at Lunham Avenue.

Introduction
Early settlers recognized the importance of setting aside sections of lakefront for future Milwaukeeans. South of Milwau-

kee proper, residents of St. Francis, Cudahy, and South Milwaukee are fortunate to have a string of county parks along Lake Michigan. Not to suggest that they're the only ones to enjoy these green spaces, for people come from all around greater Milwaukee to bike, jog, walk, cross-country ski, swim, sun, picnic, and play in these bluff-side parks.

Sheridan, Warnimont, and Grant Parks join in a continuous line from the north end in Cudahy at 4300 South to Oak Creek Parkway in South Milwaukee at 7500 South. **The walk begins right at the place where South Lake Drive and Lunham Avenue meet and the Kiwanis Club welcomes you to Cudahy, "Tree City USA." Head south to enter Sheridan Park and step onto the bike trail.** Watch carefully for Lycra-garbed mountain bikers out for some serious sweaty exercise who, correctly, believe they own the right-of-way on this trail. They don't exactly own it, but this is a designated bike trail, complete with a center line, and their speed machines command respect. The walk is well worth the risk.

There's not much to see and do here. This is a "lake walk," a meander, meant to be taken slowly while enjoying the daily mood of Lake Michigan. This is a place to lie down on the bluff, listen to waves below, and make up silly stories about lazy clouds above.

On a hot day, "cooler by the lake" takes on tactile meaning, and the view of the lake is spectacularly gentle. When prevailing western breezes push whitecaps eastward, the lake will often be arranged in alternating bands of navy blue and turquoise. Photographers will find it impossible to capture; you have to be there to feel the wind on your face while the lake paints patterns that bend and ripple.

At the intersection just below the playground, turn left

and walk down the bluff. Several switchbacks on the path will take you to a sandy beach. Here a series of concrete piers provide a place to rest while lake mist supplies on-the-spot air conditioning.

The bluff to the south looks as if Bigfoot has been nibbling at it. Let's hope this process won't claim these lakefront parks. So far the missing chunks haven't done any crucial damage to the park system, and other than a number of warnings at the top about not getting too close to the edge, the changing topography hasn't affected use of the lakefront.

It's not unusual on a lazy summer day to find little Huckleberry Finns clutching bags of marshmallows and collecting driftwood for an afternoon adventure. Soon the smell of burning sugar and woodsmoke will blow your way, along with forgotten childhood dreams.

To make sure visitors don't forget where they are, a stream of inbound planes headed for Mitchell Field follows a landing pattern over the lake. **After a leisurely return up the bluff, continue walking south to the place where the trail crosses the road. Turn around here and head backwards to complete this two-mile round-trip walk.**

If you're thirsty and hungry afterward and it's Monday, you might want to drive south on Lake Drive to the Fountain Blue, a Polish restaurant at 5133 South Lake Drive for a cool drink and a memorable Polish buffet. You won't be disappointed. This writer was there the night (then) vice presidential candidate Dan Quayle dropped in with Senator Bob Kasten, an army of Secret Service personnel, and an entourage of media people. Look for the plaque on the wall designating the table where the dignitaries dined.

No. 20 Wauwatosa Walk

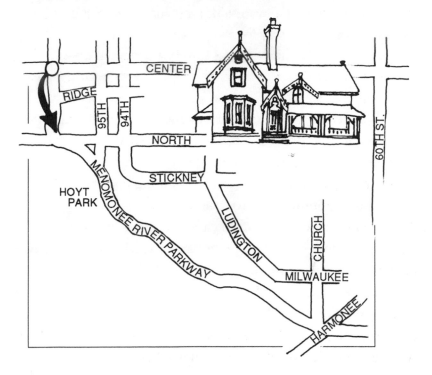

Distance
4.5 miles

How to Begin
Take Highway 100 north from I-94 West to North Avenue.
Follow North Avenue east to Menomonee River Parkway, turn
left, and drive to the corner of the Parkway and Center Street.

Introduction
The main bulk of Wauwatosa looks like a square bagel with
the Milwaukee County Institution grounds making a hole in
the center and a nibble on the south side taken away by a

finger of Milwaukee proper. Actually, it's a peninsula bordered by Milwaukee on three sides while facing Brookfield and Elm Grove to the west. Wauwatosa doesn't like to reveal its character all at once, but stay for awhile and this center of dichotomies and wig stores might reveal some unexpected charm.

A walk here can be fraught with danger if you don't step carefully into the street and stop, look, and listen at every intersection. Fortunately, at most corners a stop sign commands racing motorists to pause, thus giving pedestrians a window of opportunity to cross safely.

A tour of inner Wauwatosa can be accomplished by **starting at the corner of Center Street and the Menomonee River Parkway and following the Parkway into the village, pride of Wauwatosa.**

A word about the Menomonee River. It bubbles diagonally across Wauwatosa traveling northwest to southeast surrounded by green space that lends itself to picnics and lovers. The murky shallow water might remind you of a comment recorded from the words of Captain John Hance on the subject of the Colorado River before it was dammed.

According to Hance, "Too thick to drink and too thin to plow. One day I stooped to drink, and the mud was . . . thick. I tried to bite the water off, but my teeth were bad. Finally, I managed to pull my trusty knife out of my boot and cut off the water." That's the Menomonee.

When you get to North Avenue, take a deep breath, bolt at the "walk" signal and if you're quick, you'll get halfway across before "don't walk" flashes a warning. Heed it.

From North Avenue, the Parkway enters Hoyt Park and drops you off at Harmonee Avenue. Turn left at the light, cut through a parking lot, and step into La Boulangerie at

1425 Underwood Avenue for simple gourmet fare and a welcome respite from the rigors of a four and one-half mile Wauwatosa walk.

From La Boulangerie, walk back to the Parkway the way you came and turn right on Church Street to view the First Congregational Church. This classic, early twentieth century church has all the appointments of early wealth from red bricks accented with snow-white shutters to stately pillars and a four-layered steeple set on a brick base.

Next door, the Thomas Benjamin Hart home, listed on the National Register of Historic Places, shows Gothic revival architecture and stands as the oldest house on the oldest residential street in the village. Hart operated saw and grist mills in the 1870s.

Across the street dwell two quaint "painted ladies," all dressed in tan and rust with green, gold, and blue ornamentation. They're happy-looking.

Turn left on Milwaukee Avenue to find the "Sunnyhill Home" built by Dr. Fisk Holbrook Day in 1874. Dr. Day practiced medicine at County Hospital, the Poor Farm, and the Insane Asylum. Those institutions paid Dr. Day more than minimum wage, for his place is not shabby, and like the Hart home, is registered on the National Historic Register.

From here, turn right on Ludington Avenue, left on Stickney Avenue, follow Stickney until it turns into 94th street, jog left on North Avenue, then right on 95th street, left on Ridge, and right on the Parkway back to the start, where you can decide if Wauwatosa revealed its charms on this walk.

"After the snow melted and the buyers discovered
that the land they'd purchased could be reached
only by using diving gear, it was too late to move
Milwaukee to a better location on higher ground.
Instead, the high ground was moved into the
swamp, filling up the great Milwaukee bog, and
bringing closer a day when it was possible to move
freely through the downtown district without using
the butterfly stroke. . . ."

This Is Milwaukee, *Robert W. Wells, 1970*